英语经典美文赏读与写作

陈 斌◎编著

沈阳出版发行集团
沈阳出版社

图书在版编目（CIP）数据

英语经典美文赏读与写作/陈斌编著. --沈阳：沈阳出版社，2024.10. --ISBN 978-7-5716-4134-4

Ⅰ. H319.39

中国国家版本馆 CIP 数据核字第 2024QU8780 号

出版发行：沈阳出版发行集团｜沈阳出版社
（地址：沈阳市沈河区南翰林路 10 号　邮编：110011）
网　　址：http://www.sycbs.com
印　　刷：北京四海锦诚印刷技术有限公司
幅面尺寸：170mm×240mm
印　　张：12.75
字　　数：240千字
出版时间：2025 年 3 月第 1 版
印刷时间：2025 年 3 月第 1 次印刷
责任编辑：吕　晶
责任校对：高玉君
责任监印：杨　旭

书　　号：ISBN 978-7-5716-4134-4
定　　价：88.00 元

联系电话：024-24112447
E‐mail：sy24112447@163.com

本书若有印装质量问题，影响阅读，请与出版社联系调换。

Preface

There is no denying that we people can get abundant information we need from different channels. But here I strongly recommend a traditional one, which is reading classics. Here are two reasons for it. On the one hand, it is a good way for us to broaden our horizon and increase our knowledge in many aspects. On the other hand, it is also a chance for us to enhance our aesthetic taste, for most of them have very special language styles, which will give us readers more enjoyment and interest.

However, nowadays a large number of people, especially the young, are unwilling to or cannot spend their time in reading classics. There are some reasons accounting for the phenomenon and I would like to state two of them. For one thing, people are distracted by other things increasingly, which can give them more joy and fun and have no requirement in thinking, such as all kinds of entertainment activities. For another, some people think that it is no use reading classics because these classics are out of date and useless to our lives, let alone to our society.

In my opinion, it is wrong to consider classics as an outdated matter because it still has many important functions and influences on our society and our lives. Classics are a kind of treasure in a nation and a culture.

This book is a collection of forty classical articles, which cover many aspects of our life. While reading, we are bound to find that they are charming and attractive. And after reading, there are also some tasks for you to help you better understand each classic and express your personal opinion about it. And I am sure that after a period, we can imitate some wonderful sentence patterns in our own passage, blurt out a beautiful paragraph and even deliver an excellent speech.

All in all, we can benefit a lot from reading classics. Let's start from today and get to read classics!

前　言

　　随着社会的不断进步和信息技术的持续发展，读者可以从多种渠道获取海量信息和进行阅读。在这样的趋势之下，一种传统的阅读方式仍然深受人们的喜欢。在众多的阅读内容之中，英文经典文章一直受到广大读者的青睐。探寻其原因，有三个方面：首先，阅读英文经典文章能够帮助我们提高英语阅读能力和丰富英语语言知识。其次，阅读英文经典文章可以帮助我们提升审美情趣和浸润心灵。最后，阅读英文经典文章促使我们更好地理解外国文化和拓宽国际视野。

　　本书就是为了满足广大读者对于阅读英文经典文章的需求而创作的。全书共分为两部分，选取了40篇英文经典文章，其中包含32篇经典美文和8篇名人演讲，每篇文章包含读前导语、美文欣赏、词汇释义、难句解析、参考译文和读后写作六个部分，共计二十余万字，由陈斌独立编著完成。希望能为喜爱阅读英文经典文章的读者提供阅读和写作的帮助。

　　限于编者水平有限，加之时间紧促，书中疏漏和不足之处在所难免，欢迎各位专家、读者批评指正。

编者
2024年10月

目 录

Part I Beautiful Articles Sharing
第一部分 美文分享回味时刻

1 Youth
    青 春 ——Samuel Ullman （3）

2 If I Rest, I Rust
    如果我休息，我就会生锈 ——Orisen Marden （6）

3 Companionship of Books
    以书为伴 ——Samuel Smiles （10）

4 Three Days to See
    假如给我三天光明 ——Helen Keller （15）

5 An October Sunrise
    十月的日出 ——Richard D. Blackmore （21）

6 Born to Win
    生而为赢 ——Horatio Alger （25）

7 The Road to Success
    成功之道 ——Andrew Carnegie （30）

8 Nature
    自 然 ——Ralph Waldo Emerson （35）

9 How to Read a Good Book ——John Ruskin (40)
   怎样读一本好书

10 Human Life Like a Poem ——Lin Yutang (44)
   人生如诗

11 Beautiful Smile and Love ——Mother Teresa (49)
   美丽的微笑与爱心

12 Mirror, Mirror—What do I See? ——Derek Walcott (54)
   镜子，镜子，告诉我

13 On Immortality in Youth ——William Hazlitt (58)
   论青春之不朽

14 On Motes and Beams ——William Somerset Maugham (62)
   微尘与栋梁

15 Man and Nature ——Hamilton Wright Mabie (66)
   人与自然

16 Three Passions in My Life ——Bertrand Russell (70)
   我生命中的三种激情

17 The Delights of Reading ——Sir John Lubbock (74)
   读书之乐

18 The Happy Door ——Mildred Cram (78)
   快乐之门

19 The Love of Beauty ——John Ruskin (82)
   爱　美

20 The Man in Old Age ——Bertrand Russell (86)
   人生之暮年

21	The True Nobility 真正的高贵	——Ernest Hemingway	(89)
22	We Are on a Journey 人在旅途	——Henry Van Dyke	(92)
23	Work and Pleasure 工作和娱乐	——Winston Churchill	(95)
24	What is Your Recovery Rate? 你的恢复速率是多少?	——Graham Harris	(99)
25	Be Happy! 活得快乐!	——Lloyd Morris	(103)
26	To Be or Not to Be 生存或者毁灭	——William Lyon Phelps	(107)
27	On Beauty 论　美	——Kahlil Gibran	(111)
28	Summer Sunrises on the Mississippi 密西西比河上夏天的日出	——Mark Twain	(115)
29	Choice of Companions 择　友	——William Thackeray	(119)
30	When Love Beckons You 爱的召唤	——Kahlil Gibran	(123)
31	On Meeting the Celebrated 论见名人	——W. S. Maugham	(127)
32	The Faculty of Delight 喜悦的力量	——Charles Edward Montague	(131)

Part II Wonderful Celebrity Speeches
第二部分 名人演讲精彩瞬间

33 Gettysburg Address
　　葛底斯堡演说 —— Abraham Lincoln （137）

34 I Have a Dream（Excerpts）
　　我有一个梦想（节选） —— Martin Luther King JR （141）

35 First Inaugural Address of John F. Kennedy（Excerpts）
　　肯尼迪总统就职演说（节选）
　　　　　　　　　　　　　　　　　　　—— John F. Kennedy （148）

36 First Inaugural Address of Franklin D. Roosevelt
　　罗斯福总统就职演说
　　　　　　　　　　　　　　　　　—— Franklin D. Roosevelt （153）

37 Blood, Toil, Tears and Sweat
　　带着血泪和汗水抗争到底 —— Winston Churchill （164）

38 Arm Yourselves and Be Ye Men of Valour
　　鼓起勇气 —— Winston Churchill （170）

39 We Shall Fight on the Beaches（Excerpts）
　　我们将战斗到底（节选） —— Winston Churchill （179）

40 The World As I See It
　　我的世界观 —— Albert Einstein （186）

Part I
Beautiful Articles Sharing
第一部分　美文分享回味时刻

Youth
青　春
——Samuel Ullman

读前导语

　　本篇文章作者塞缪尔·厄尔曼（1840—1924）是美国作家，1840年出生于德国，儿时随家人移居美国，参加过南北战争，之后定居伯明翰，经营五金杂货，年逾70开始写作，本篇文章是他的代表作。

　　他在文中写道："青春不是年华，而是心境；青春不是桃面、朱唇、柔膝，而是深沉的意志、无限的遐想和炙热的恋情；青春如生命的深泉在涌流。"

美文欣赏

　　Youth is not a time of life; it is a state of mind; it is not a matter of rosy① cheeks, red lips and supple② knees; it is a matter of the will, a quality of the imagination, a vigor③ of the emotions; it is the freshness of the deep springs of life.

　　Youth means a temperamental④ predominance⑤ of courage over timidity⑥, of the appetite⑦ for adventure over the love of ease. This often exists in a man of 60 more than a boy of 20. Nobody grows old merely by a number of years. We grow old by deserting⑧ our ideals.

　　Years may wrinkle⑨ the skin, but to give up enthusiasm⑩ wrinkles the soul. Worry, fear, self-distrust bows the heart and turns the spirit back to dust.

　　Whether 60 or 16, there is in every human being's heart the lure⑪ of wonders, the unfailing appetite for what's next, and the joy of the game of living. In the center of your heart and my heart, there is a wireless station; so long as it receives messages of beauty, hope, courage and power from man and from the infinite⑫, so long as you are young.

When your aerials⑬ are down, and your spirit is covered with snows of cynicism⑭ and the ice of pessimism⑮, then you've grown old, even at 20; but as long as your aerials are up, to catch waves of optimism⑯, there's hope you may die young at 80.

词汇释义

① **rosy** ['rəʊzi] *adj.* 玫瑰色的；愉快的，乐观的

② **supple** ['sʌpl] *adj.* 灵活的；柔韧性好的

③ **vigor** ['vɪɡə] *n.* 活力；热情

④ **temperamental** [ˌteɪmprə'mentl] *adj.* 性格的；性情的

⑤ **predominance** [prɪ'dɒmɪnəns] *n.* 优势；主导地位

⑥ **timidity** [tɪ'mɪdəti] *n.* 胆怯，羞怯；小心翼翼；怯懦

⑦ **appetite** ['æpɪtaɪt] *n.* 胃口，食欲；强烈欲望

⑧ **desert** [dɪ'zɜːt] *v.* 遗弃，离弃，放弃；擅离职守

⑨ **wrinkle** ['rɪŋkl] *v.* 使起皱纹

⑩ **enthusiasm** [ɪn'θjuːziæzəm] *n.* 热情，热忱；热衷的事物

⑪ **lure** [lʊə(r)] *n.* 有诱惑力的人（或物）

⑫ **infinite** ['ɪnfɪnət] *adj.* 无数的，不计其数的；极其的；无限的

⑬ **aerial** ['eəriəl] *n.* 天线 *adj.* 空中的

⑭ **cynicism** ['sɪnɪsɪzəm] *n.* 认为世人皆自私的观念；愤世嫉俗

⑮ **pessimism** ['pesɪmɪzəm] *n.* 悲观；悲观情绪；悲观主义

⑯ **optimism** ['ɒptɪmɪzəm] *n.* 乐观；乐观主义

难句解析

1. Youth means a temperamental predominance of courage over timidity, of the appetite for adventure over the love of ease.

[译文] 青春气贯长虹，勇锐盖过怯弱，进取压倒苟安。

[解析] "predominance" 这里指的是 "优势，占主导地位的事物"，"the appetite for" 本意为 "对……的欲望"，此处可以翻译成 "渴望"。

2. When your aerials are down, and your spirit is covered with snows of cynicism and the ice of pessimism, then you've grown old, even at 20; but as long as your aerials are up, to catch waves of optimism, there's hope you may die young at 80.

[译文] 一旦天线下降，锐气便被冰雪覆盖，玩世不恭、自暴自弃油然而生，即使年方二十，实已垂垂老矣；然则只是竖起天线，捕捉乐观信号，你就有望在八十高龄告别尘寰时仍觉青春相伴左右。

[解析] 文中的"down"与"up"相对，"snows of cynicism and the ice of pessimism"与"waves of optimism"，用对比的方式写出了青春不在于人本身的年龄，而在于人的心态与志向。

参考译文

青 春

青春不是年华，而是心境；青春不是桃面、朱唇、柔膝，而是深沉的意志、无限的遐想和炙热的感情；青春如生命的深泉在涌流。

青春气贯长虹，勇锐盖过怯弱，进取压倒苟安。如此锐气，二十后生而有之，六旬老者更多见。年岁有加，并非垂老；理想丢弃，方堕暮年。

岁月悠悠，于肌肤上显露印记；热忱抛却，颓废必至灵魂。烦忧、惶恐、丧失自信，定使心灵扭曲，意气如灰。

无论年届花甲，抑或二八芳龄，心中皆有奇迹之诱惑、孩童般的好奇以及生命之欢乐。人人心中皆有无线电台，只要它从天上人间接受美好、希望、欢乐、勇气和力量的信号，你就青春永驻。

一旦天线下降，锐气便被冰雪覆盖，玩世不恭、自暴自弃油然而生，即使年方二十，实已垂垂老矣；然则只是竖起天线，捕捉乐观信号，你就有望在八十高龄告别尘寰时仍觉青春相伴左右。

读后写作

Youth is a lively topic. Youth is a mature turning. What is your opinion about "Youth"?

If I Rest, I Rust
如果我休息，我就会生锈
——Orison Marden

读前导语

本篇文章作者奥里森·马登（1848—1924），被公认为美国成功学的奠基人和最伟大的成功励志导师，成功学之父。他撰写了大量鼓舞人心的著作，包括《人生的资本》《思考与成功》《伟大的励志书》《成功的品质》等。他创办了《成功》杂志，该杂志通过创造性地传播成功学，改变了无数美国人的命运。本篇文章是他的代表作之一。

他在文中写道："甚至最为勤勉的人也以此作为警示：如果一个人有才能而不用，就像废弃钥匙上的铁一样，这些才能就会很快生锈，并最终无法完成安排给自己的工作。"

美文欣赏

The significant inscription[①] found on an old key— "If I rest, I rust" —would be an excellent motto for those who are afflicted[②] with the slightest bit of idleness[③]. Even the most industrious[④] person might adopt it with advantage to serve as a reminder that, if one allows his faculties[⑤] to rest, like the iron in the unused key, they will soon show signs of rust and, ultimately[⑥], cannot do the work required of them.

Those who would attain[⑦] the heights reached and kept by great men must keep their faculties polished[⑧] by constant use, so that they may unlock the doors of knowledge, the gate that guard the entrances to the professions, to science, art, literature, agriculture—every department of human endeavor[⑨].

Industry keeps bright the key that opens the treasury of achievement. If Hugh Miller, after toiling⑩ all day in a quarry⑪, had devoted his evenings to rest and recreation, he would never have become a famous geologist. The celebrated mathematician, Edmund Stone, would never have published a mathematical dictionary, never have found the key to science of mathematics, if he had given his spare moments to idleness, had the little Scotch lad, Ferguson, allowed the busy brain to go to sleep while he tended sheep on the hillside instead of calculating the position of the stars by a string of beads, he would never have become a famous astronomer⑫.

Labor vanquishes⑬ all—not inconstant⑭, spasmodic⑮, or ill-directed labor; but faithful, unremitting⑯, daily effort toward a well-directed purpose. Just as truly as eternal vigilance⑰ is the price of liberty, so is eternal industry the price of noble and enduring success.

词汇释义

①**inscription** [ɪnˈskrɪpʃ(ə)n] n. 题字，碑铭

②**afflict** [əˈflɪkt] v. 使苦恼，折磨

③**idleness** [ˈaɪdlnəs] n. 懒惰，闲散，失业

④**industrious** [ɪnˈdʌstriəs] adj. 勤劳的，勤奋的，勤恳的

⑤**faculty** [ˈfæk(ə)lti] n. 才能，能力；全体教员

⑥**ultimately** [ˈʌltɪmətli] adv. 最后，最终；基本上；根本

⑦**attain** [əˈteɪn] v. 获得；达到

⑧**polish** [ˈpɒlɪʃ] n. 光泽，优雅，精良 v. 擦亮，磨光，推敲

⑨**endeavor** [ɪnˈdevə] n. 努力，尽力

⑩**toil** [tɔɪl] n. 辛苦，苦工；网，罗网，圈套 v. 苦干，跋涉

⑪**quarry** [ˈkwɒri] n. 采石场；猎获物；出处

⑫**astronomer** [əˈstrɒnəmə(r)] n. 天文学家

⑬**vanquish** [ˈvæŋkwɪʃ] vt. 征服；战胜；克服；抑制

⑭**inconstant** [ɪnˈkɒnstənt] adj. （感情）易变的，无常的；常变的

⑮**spasmodic** [spæzˈmɒdɪk] adj. 痉挛的；一阵阵的

⑯**unremitting** [ˌʌnrɪˈmɪtɪŋ] adj. 不歇的，不断的，坚忍的

⑰**vigilance** [ˈvɪdʒɪləns] n. 警戒，警觉心

难句解析

1. Those who would attain the heights reached and kept by great men must keep their faculties polished by constant use, so that they may unlock the doors of knowledge, the gate that guard the entrances to the professions, to science, art, literature, agriculture—every department of human endeavor.

译文 有些人想取得伟人所获得并保持的成就，他们就必须不断运用自身才能，以便开启知识的大门，即那些通往人类努力探求的各个领域的大门，这些领域包括各种职业：科学、艺术、文学、农业等。

解析 "reached and kept by great men"是过去分词作定语，修饰"heights"，这里的"faculties"意思是"才能"。

2. If Hugh Miller, after toiling all day in a quarry, had devoted his evenings to rest and recreation, he would never have become a famous geologist.

译文 如果休·米勒在采石场劳作一天后，晚上的时光用来休息消遣的话，他就不会成为名垂青史的地质学家。

解析 这句话的主干是"If Hugh Miller… had devoted…, he would never…"。

参考译文

如果我休息，我就会生锈

一把旧钥匙上镌刻了一则意义深远的铭文——如果我休息了，我就会生锈。对于那些懒散而烦恼的人来说，这将是至理名言。甚至最为勤勉的人也以此作为警示：如果一个人有才能而不用，就像废弃钥匙上的铁一样，这些才能就会很快生锈，并最终无法完成安排给自己的工作。

有些人想取得伟人所获得并保持的成就，他们就必须不断运用自身才能，以便开启知识的大门，即那些通往人类努力探求的各个领域的大门，这些领域包括各种职业：科学、艺术、文学、农业等。

勤奋使开启成功宝库的钥匙保持光亮。如果休·米勒在采石场劳作一天后，晚上的时光用来休息消遣的话，他就不会成为名垂青史的地质学家。著名数学家埃德蒙·斯通如果闲暇时无所事事，就不会出版数学词典，也不会发现开启数学之门的钥匙。如果苏格兰青年弗格森在山坡上放羊时，让他那思维活跃的大脑处于休息状态，而不是借助一串珠子计算星星的位置，他就不会成为著名的天文学家。

劳动征服一切。这里所指的劳动不是断断续续的、间歇性的或方向偏差的劳动，而是坚定的、不懈的、方向正确的每日劳动。正如要想拥有自由就要时刻保持警惕一样，要想取得伟大的、持久的成功，就必须坚持不懈地努力。

读后写作

Today some people want to live a comfortable life without struggling, while others fight for a better life without any stop. What is your choice after reading the passage?

Companionship of Books
以书为伴
——Samuel Smiles

读前导语

本篇文章作者塞缪尔·斯迈尔斯（1812—1904），英国19世纪道德学家、社会改革家和散文随笔作家。他一生写过20多部作品，其中最受欢迎的是有关人生成功与幸福，有关良知、信仰、道德、自由与责任等领域的随笔作品。本篇文章就是他的代表作之一。

他在文中写道："好书就像是你最好的朋友。它始终不渝，过去如此，现在如此，将来也永远不变。它是最有耐心、最令人愉悦的伴侣。在我们穷愁潦倒、临危遭难时，它也不会抛弃我们，对我们总是一如既往地亲切。"

美文欣赏

A man may usually be known by the books he reads as well as by the company[①] he keeps; for there is a companionship[②] of books as well as of men; and one should always live in the best company, whether it be of books or of men.

A good book may be among the best of friends. It is the same today that it always was, and it will never change. It is the most patient and cheerful[③] of companions. It does not turn its back upon us in times of adversity[④] or distress. It always receives us with the same kindness; amusing and instructing[⑤] us in youth, and comforting and consoling[⑥] us in age.

Men often discover their affinity⑦ to each other by the mutual love they have for a book just as two persons sometimes discover a friend by the admiration which both entertain for a third. There is an old proverb⑧, "Love me, love my dog." But there is more wisdom in this: "Love me, love my book." The book is a truer and higher bond of union. Men can think, feel, and sympathize with each other through their favorite author. They live in him together, and he in them.

A good book is often the best urn of a life enshrining⑨ the best that life could think out; for the world of a man's life is, for the most part, but the world of his thoughts. Thus the best books are treasuries⑩ of good words, the golden thoughts, which, remembered and cherished⑪, become our constant companions and comforters.

Books possess an essence⑫ of immortality⑬. They are by far the most lasting products of human effort. Temples and statues decay⑭, but books survive. Time is of no account with great thoughts, which are as fresh today as when they first passed through their author's minds, ages ago. What was then said and thought still speaks to us as vividly as ever from the printed page. The only effect of time has been to sift⑮ out the bad products; for nothing in literature can long survive but what is really good.

Books introduce us into the best society; they bring us into the presence of the greatest minds that have ever lived. We hear what they said and did; we see them as if they were really alive; we sympathize⑯ with them, enjoy with them, grieve⑰ with them; their experience becomes ours, and we feel as if we were in a measure actors with them in the scenes which they describe.

The great and good do not die, even in this world. Embalmed⑱ in books, their spirits walk abroad. The book is a living voice. It is an intellect to which one still listens.

词汇释义

①**company** [ˈkʌmpəni] *n.* 陪伴；宾客；在一起的一群人

②**companionship** [kəmˈpænjənʃɪp] *n.* 友谊；伴侣关系

③**cheerful** ［ˈtʃɪəfl］ *adj.* 高兴的，兴高采烈的

④**adversity** ［ədˈvɜːsəti］ *n.* 困境，逆境

⑤**instruct** ［ɪnˈstrʌkt］ *vt.* 教，讲授；教导，指导；通知；命令

⑥**console** ［kənˈsəʊl］ *v.* 安慰，慰问

⑦**affinity** ［əˈfɪnəti］ *n.* 密切关系，姻亲关系

⑧**proverb** ［ˈprɒvɜːb］ *n.* 谚语，格言

⑨**enshrine** ［ɪnˈʃraɪn］ *vt.* 珍藏，铭记；把……奉为神圣；秘藏

⑩**treasury** ［ˈtreʒəri］ *n.* 国库，金库；（政府的）财政部

⑪**cherish** ［ˈtʃerɪʃ］ *v.* 珍惜；怀念（过去），抱有（希望）

⑫**essence** ［ˈesns］ *n.* 本质，精髓；精油；香精

⑬**immortality** ［ˌɪmɔːˈtæləti］ *n.* 不朽，不朽的声名

⑭**decay** ［dɪˈkeɪ］ *v.* （使）腐烂，腐朽；衰败 *n.* 腐烂，腐朽；衰败

⑮**sift** ［sɪft］ *v.* 筛分；精选；撒；审查

⑯**sympathize** ［ˈsɪmpəθaɪz］ *v.* 同情，怜悯；共鸣，同感

⑰**grieve** ［griːv］ *v.* 伤心；悲伤

⑱**embalm** ［ɪmˈbɑːm］ *vt.* 保存（尸体）不腐；使不被遗忘

难句解析

1. A man may usually be known by the books he reads as well as by the company he keeps; for there is a companionship of books as well as of men;…

译文 通常看一个人读些什么书就可知道他的为人，就像看他同什么人交往就可知道他的为人一样，因为有人以人为伴，也有人以书为伴。

解析 be known by…译为"被……所知"，as well as…译为"也，和"，keep…company 译为"与……相伴"。A man may usually be known by the books he reads as well as by the company he keeps…"he reads"和"he keeps"分别作"the books"和"the company"的定语。

2. Books introduce us into the best society; they bring us into the presence of the

greatest minds that have ever lived.

[译文] 书籍介绍我们与最优秀的人为伍，使我们置身于历代伟人巨匠之间。

[解析] introduce ... into 和 bring ... into 形成呼应，that have ever lived 充当 the greatest minds 的定语，将书籍能给我们带来的好处表达得完整而丰富。

参考译文

以书为伴

通常看一个人读些什么书就可知道他的为人，就像看他同什么人交往就可知道他的为人一样，因为有人以人为伴，也有人以书为伴。无论是书友还是朋友，我们都应该以最好的为伴。

好书就像是你最好的朋友。它始终不渝，过去如此，现在如此，将来也永远不变。它是最有耐心、最令人愉悦的伴侣。在我们穷愁潦倒、临危遭难时，它也不会抛弃我们，对我们总是一如既往地亲切。在我们年轻时，好书陶冶我们的性情，增长我们的知识；到我们年老时，它又给我们以慰藉和勉励。

人们常常因为喜欢同一本书而结为知己，就像有时两个人因为敬慕同一个人而成为朋友一样。有句古谚说道："爱屋及乌。"其实"爱我及书"这句话蕴含更多的哲理。书是更为真诚而高尚的情谊纽带。人们可以通过共同喜爱的作家沟通思想，交流感情，彼此息息相通，并与自己喜欢的作家思想相通，情感相融。

好书常如最精美的宝器，珍藏着人生的思想的精华，因为人生的境界主要就在于其思想的境界。因此，最好的书是金玉良言和崇高思想的宝库，这些良言和思想若铭记于心并多加珍视，就会成为我们忠实的伴侣和永恒的慰藉。

书籍具有不朽的本质，是人类努力创造的最为持久的成果。寺庙会倒塌，神像会朽烂，而书却经久长存。对于伟大的思想来说，时间是无关紧要的。多年前初次出现于脑海的宏大思想今日仍然清爽如故。他们当时的言论和思想刊于书页，如今仍旧那么生动感人。时间唯一的作用是淘汰不好的作品，因为只有真正的佳作才能经世长存。

书籍介绍我们与最优秀的人为伍，使我们置身于历代伟人巨匠之间，如闻其声，如观其行，如见其人，同他们情感交融，悲喜与共，感同身受。我们觉得自己仿佛在作者所描绘的舞台上和他们一起登场。

即使在人世间，伟大杰出的人物也永生不老。他们的精神被载入书册，传于四海。书是人生至今仍在聆听的智慧之声，永远充满着活力。

读后写作

As is written in the passage, books are the most faithful friends to us. Can you introduce one of your favorite books to us?

Three Days to See
假如给我三天光明
——Helen Keller

读前导语

本篇文章作者海伦·凯勒（1880—1968），是美国著名作家、教育家、慈善家、社会活动家。她在出生十九个月时因猩红热被夺去了视力和听力。她的生命有87年是在无光、无声的世界中度过的。本篇文章就是她的代表作之一。

她在书中写道："习惯于光明的人或许根本无法理解处于黑暗的人们的心中的痛苦，所以他也不会珍惜光明；同样，每天有着丰富的机会去进行观察的人反而失去了用心生活的乐趣，无法从周围接触的事物中得到对生活最根本的享受。"

美文欣赏

All of us have read thrilling[1] stories in which the hero had only a limited and specified time to live. Sometimes it was as long as a year, sometimes as short as 24 hours. But always we were interested in discovering just how the doomed[2] hero chose to spend his last days or his last hours. I speak, of course, of free men who have a choice, not condemned[3] criminals whose sphere of activities is strictly delimited.

Such stories set us thinking, wondering what we should do under similar circumstances[4]. What events, what experiences, what associations should we crowd into those last hours as mortal beings? What happiness should we find in reviewing the past? What regrets?

Sometimes I have thought it would be an excellent rule to live each day as if we should die tomorrow. Such an attitude would emphasize sharply the values of life. We should live each day with gentleness, vigor and a keenness of appreciation which are often lost when time stretches⑤ before us in the constant panorama⑥ of more days and months and years to come. There are those, of course, who would adopt the Epicurean motto of "Eat, drink, and be merry". But most people would be chastened by the certainty of impending⑦ death.

In stories the doomed⑧ hero is usually saved at the last minute by some stroke of fortune, but almost always his sense of values is changed. He becomes more appreciative⑨ of the meaning of life and its permanent⑩ spiritual values. It has often been noted that those who live, or have lived, in the shadow of death bring a mellow sweetness to everything they do.

Most of us, however, take life for granted. We know that one day we must die, but usually we picture that day as far in the future. When we are in buoyant⑪ health, death is all but unimaginable. We seldom think of it. The days stretch out in an endless vista. So we go about our petty tasks, hardly aware of our listless attitude toward life.

The same lethargy⑫, I am afraid, characterizes the use of all our faculties and senses. Only the deaf appreciate hearing, only the blind realize the manifold blessings that lie in sight. Particularly does this observation apply to those who have lost sight and hearing in adult life. But those who have never suffered impairment⑬ of sight or hearing seldom make the fullest use of these blessed faculties. Their eyes and ears take in all sights and sounds hazily, without concentration and with little appreciation. It is the same old story of not being grateful for what we have until we lose it, of not being conscious of health until we are ill.

I have often thought it would be a blessing if each human being were stricken blind and deaf for a few days at some time during his early adult life. Darkness would make him more appreciative of sight; silence would teach him the joys of sound.

Now and then I have tested my seeing friends to discover what they see. Recently I was visited by a very good friend who had just returned from a long walk in the woods, and I asked her what she had observed. "Nothing in particular," she replied. I might have been incredulous⑭ had I not been accustomed to such responses, for long ago I became convinced that the seeing see little.

How was it possible, I asked myself, to walk for an hour through the woods and see nothing worthy of note? I who cannot see find hundreds of things to interest me through mere touch. I feel the delicate symmetry⑮ of a leaf. I pass my hands lovingly about the smooth skin of a silver birch, or the rough shaggy⑯ bark of a pine. In spring I touch the branches of trees hopefully in search of a bud, the first sign of awakening Nature after her winter's sleep. I feel the delightful, velvety texture of a flower, and discover its remarkable convolutions; and something of the miracle of Nature is revealed⑰ to me. Occasionally, if I am very fortunate, I place my hand gently in a small tree and feel the happy quiver of a bird in full song. I am delighted to have cool waters of a brook rush through my open fingers. To me a lush carpet of pine needles or spongy⑱ grass is more welcome than the most luxurious Persian rug. To me the pageant⑲ of seasons is a thrilling and unending drama, the action of which streams through my finger tips. At times my heart cries out with longing to see all these things. If I can get so much pleasure from mere touch, how much more beauty must be revealed by sight. Yet, those who have eyes apparently see little. The panorama of color and action fill the world is taken for granted. It is human, perhaps, to appreciate little that which we have and to long for that which we have not, but it is a great pity that in the world of light the gift of sight is used only as mere convenience rather than as a means of adding fullness to life.

Oh, the things that I should see if I had the power of sight for three days!

词汇释义

① **thrilling** [ˈθrɪlɪŋ] *adj.* 令人兴奋的；毛骨悚然的；颤动的

② **doomed** [duːmd] *adj.* 注定失败（或灭亡、毁灭）的

③ **condemned** [kənˈdemd] *adj.* 被责难的，受谴责的

④ **circumstance** [ˈsɜːkəmstəns] *n.* 条件；环境；情况；情形

⑤ **stretch** [stretʃ] *v.* 伸出，伸长；拉伸

⑥ **panorama** [ˌpænəˈrɑːmə] *n.* 全景

⑦ **impending** [ɪmˈpendɪŋ] *adj.* 即将发生的；迫切的；悬挂的

⑧ **doomed** [duːmd] *adj.* 命中注定的；难逃一死的

⑨ **appreciative** [əˈpriːʃətɪv] *adj.* 欣赏的；感激的

⑩ **permanent** [ˈpɜː(r)mənənt] *adj.* 长久的；永久的，永恒的

⑪ **buoyant** [ˈbɔɪənt] *adj.* 能浮起的

⑫**lethargy** [ˈleθə(r)dʒi] *n.* 无精打采；冷漠；没有热情

⑬**impairment** [ɪmˈpeəmənt] *n.* 损害，损伤

⑭**incredulous** [ɪnˈkredjələs] *adj.* 表示怀疑的，不相信的

⑮**symmetry** [ˈsɪmətri] *n.* 对称（性）；匀称

⑯**shaggy** [ˈʃægi] *adj.* （毛发）粗长而蓬乱的

⑰**reveal** [rɪˈviːl] *v.* 揭露；泄露；透露

⑱**spongy** [ˈspʌndʒi] *adj.* 海绵似的，柔软吸水的，富有弹性的

⑲**pageant** [ˈpædʒənt] *n.* 盛会；露天表演；虚饰；选美比赛

难句解析

1. We should live each day with gentleness, vigor and a keenness of appreciation which are often lost when time stretches before us in the constant panorama of more days and months and years to come.

译文 每一天我们都应该以和善的态度、充沛的精力和热情的欣赏来度过，而这些恰恰是在来日方长时往往被我们忽视的东西。

解析 "vigor" 这里指的是 "活力，精力"，"keenness" 本意为 "热心，热忱"，此处可以翻译成 "渴望"。

2. It is the same old story of not being grateful for what we have until we lose it, of not being conscious of health until we are ill.

译文 这与常说的不失去不懂得珍惜，不生病不知道健康可贵的道理是一样的。

解析 "not... until..." 译为 "直到……才……"，"be conscious of" 译为 "在意"，此处可以翻译成 "珍惜"。

3. It is human, perhaps, to appreciate little that which we have and to long for that which we have not, but it is a great pity that in the world of light the gift of sight is used only as mere convenience rather than as a means of adding fullness to life.

译文 也许不珍惜已经拥有的，想得到还没有得到的是人的特点，但是在光明的世界里只把视觉用作一种方便的工具，而不是丰富生活的工具，这是多么令人遗憾的事情啊。

解析 "to appreciate little that which we have and to long for that which we have not"画线部分为并列结构，译为"不珍惜已经拥有的，想得到还没有得到的"，"it is a great pity that…"是主语从句。"gift"一词此处可理解为"馈赠"之意。

参考译文

假如给我三天光明

我们都读过这样一些动人的故事，故事里主人公将不久于人世。长则一年，短则24小时。但是我们总是很想知道这个即将离开人世的人是决定怎样度过他最后的日子的。当然，我所指的是有权做出选择的自由人，不是那些活动范围受到严格限制的死囚。

这一类故事会使我们思考在类似的处境下，我们自己该做些什么？在那临终前的几个小时里我们会产生哪些联想？会有多少欣慰和遗憾呢？

有时我想，把每天都当作生命的最后一天来度过也不失为一个很好的生命法则。这种人生态度使人非常重视人生的价值。每一天我们都应该以和善的态度、充沛的精力和热情的欣赏来度过，而这些恰恰是在来日方长时往往被我们忽视的东西。当然，有这样一些人奉行享乐主义的座右铭——吃喝玩乐，但是大多数人却不能摆脱死亡来临的恐惧。

在许多故事中，命运已定的主人公通常在最后一分钟，由于遭遇好运而得到拯救，然而他的价值观念几乎总是改变了。他更加领悟了生命及其永恒的精神价值的意义。常常可以看到，那些活在或者曾经活在死亡阴影中的人们，对他们所做的每件事情都赋予了一种醇美香甜之感。

我们大多数人认为生命理所当然，我们明白总有一天我们会死去，但是我们常常把这一天看得非常遥远。当我们身体强壮时，死亡便成了难以想象的事情了。我们很少会考虑它。日子一天天过去，好像没有尽头。所以我们为琐事奔波，并没有意识到我们对待生活的态度是冷漠的。

我想我们在运用我们所有五官时恐怕也同样是冷漠的。只有聋人才珍惜听力，只有盲人才能认识到能见光明的幸运。对于那些成年致盲或失聪的人来说尤其如此。但是那些听力或视力从未遭受损失的人却很少充分利用这些幸运的能力，他们对所见所闻不关注、不欣赏。这与常说的不失去不懂得珍惜，不生病不知道健康可贵的道理是一样的。

我常想如果每一个人在他成年的早些时候，有几天成了聋人或盲人也不失为一件幸事。黑暗将使他更珍惜光明；沉寂将教他知道声音的乐趣。

有时我会试探我的非盲的朋友们，想知道他们看见了什么。最近我的一位非常要好的朋友来看我，她刚刚在树林里走了很长时间，我问她看见了什么。"没什么特别的。"她回答说。若不是我早已习惯了这样的回答，我也许不会轻易相信，因为很久以前我就相信了有视力的人看不见什么。

　　我问自己，在树林中走了一小时，怎么可能什么值得注意的东西都没有看到呢？而我一个盲人仅仅通过触摸就发现了数以百计的有趣的东西。我感到树叶的对称美，用手摸着白桦树光滑的树皮或是松树那粗糙的厚厚的树皮。春天里我满怀着希望触摸着树枝寻找新芽，那是大自然冬眠后醒来的第一个征象。我感到了花朵的可爱和茸茸的感觉，发现它层层叠叠地绽开着，大自然的神奇展现在我的面前。当我把手轻轻地放在一棵小树上，如果幸运的话，偶尔会感到歌唱的小鸟欢快的颤动。我会愉快地让清凉的溪水从手指间流过。对我来说，满地厚厚的松针和松软的草坪比奢华的波斯地毯更惹人喜爱。对我来说四季变换的景色如同一场动人心魄的不会完结的戏剧，剧中的人物动作从我的指尖流过。我的心不时在呐喊，带着对光明的渴望。既然仅仅通过触摸就能使我获得如此多的喜悦，那么光明定会展示更多美好的事物啊。可惜的是那些有眼睛的人分明看到很少，整个世界缤纷的色彩和万物的活动都被认为是理所当然的。也许不珍惜已经拥有的，想得到还没有得到的是人的特点，但是在光明的世界里只把视觉用作一种方便的工具，而不是丰富生活的工具，这是令人多么遗憾的事情啊。

　　噢，假如我拥有三天光明，我将会看见多少事物啊！

读后写作

　　Just as Helen Keller, if you were given three days to see in your whole life, what would you do?

An October Sunrise
十月的日出
——Richard D. Blackmore

读前导语

本篇文章作者理查德·布雷克默（1825—1900）。他是英国著名的诗人、作家、小说家。

他在文中写道："也许，那永恒的晨光就会这样降临人间，那时不再有险崖沟壑，不再有峰峦山谷，也不再有浩瀚无际的海洋；那时荣耀不会吓走幸福，幸福也不会忌妒荣耀；万物都将踊跃升腾，在造物主慈爱的光芒中生辉，因为太阳已经升起。"

美文欣赏

I was up the next morning before the October sunrise, and away through the wild and the woodland. The rising of the sun was noble in the cold and warmth of it; peeping① down the spread of light, he raised his shoulder heavily over the edge of grey mountain and wavering② length of upland. Beneath his gaze the dew-fogs dipped, and crept③ to the hollow places; then stole away in line and column, holding skirts, and clinging④ subtly at the sheltering corners where rock hung over grassland, while the brave lines of the hills came forth, one beyond other gliding.

The woods arose in folds, like drapery⑤ of awakened mountains, stately with a depth of awe, and memory of the tempests. Autumn's mellow hand was upon them, as they owned already, touched with gold and red and olive, and their joy towards the sun was less to a bridegroom than a father.

Yet before the floating impress of the woods could clear itself, suddenly the gladsome light leaped over hill and valley, casting amber, blue, and purple, and a tint of rich red rose; according to the scene they lit on, and the curtain flung⑥ around; yet all alike dispelling⑦ fear and the cloven⑧ hoof of darkness, all on the wings of hope advancing, and proclaiming⑨, "God is here!" Then life and joy sprang reassured⑩ from every crouching⑪ hollow⑫; every flower, and bud and bird had a fluttering⑬ sense of them; and all the flashing of God's gaze merged into soft beneficence⑭.

So, perhaps, shall break upon us that eternal⑮ morning, when crag⑯ and chasm⑰ shall be no more, neither hill and valley, nor great unvintaged⑱ ocean; when glory shall not scare happiness, neither happiness envy glory; but all things shall arise, and shine in the light of the Father's countenance⑲, because itself is risen.

词汇释义

①**peep** [piːp] v. 窥视，偷看

②**waver** [ˈweɪvə(r)] v. 波动；摇摆

③**creep** [kriːp] v. 缓慢行进，悄悄移动，潜行

④**cling** [klɪŋ] v. 依附，附着；抓紧，抱紧

⑤**drapery** [ˈdreɪpəri] n. 布料；打褶的帐幔

⑥**fling** [flɪŋ] v. 猛扑；猛冲；急伸

⑦**dispel** [dɪˈspel] vt. 消除；驱散；驱逐

⑧**cloven** [ˈkləʊv(ə)n] adj. 劈开的，裂开的

⑨**proclaim** [prəˈkleɪm] vt. 宣告，公布；表明；强调，声称

⑩**reassure** [ˌriːəˈʃʊə(r)] v. 使安心；使打消疑虑；安慰

⑪**crouch** [kraʊtʃ] v. 蹲下，蹲伏；蜷缩

⑫**hollow** [ˈhɒləʊ] n. 坑，洞；山谷

⑬**fluttering** [ˈflʌtərɪŋ] v. 摆动（flutter 的现在分词）

⑭**beneficence** [bɪˈnefɪs(ə)ns] n. 善行；慈善

⑮**eternal** [ɪˈtɜːn(ə)l] adj. 不朽的；永久的；永恒的；无休止的

⑯ **crag** [kræɡ] *n.* 悬崖，峭壁
⑰ **chasm** [ˈkæzəm] *n.* 峡谷；裂缝、断层；裂口；（感情等的）分歧
⑱ **vintage** [ˈvɪntɪdʒ] *n.* 酿制的酒；酿造年份 *adj.* 佳酿的；优质的
⑲ **countenance** [ˈkaʊntənəns] *n.* 面容；脸色；面部表情

难句解析

1. The woods arose in folds, like drapery of awakened mountains, stately with a depth of awe, and memory of the tempests.

译文 森林也层层叠叠地显现，宛若刚刚苏醒的山峦的斗篷，端庄威严，并带着狂风暴雨的回忆。

解析 "in folds"译为"重叠，层叠"，"awakened"译为"刚睡醒的，苏醒过来的"，"awe"译为"敬畏"，此处对于金秋十月森林的描写于温婉中流露着威严。

2. Yet before the floating impress of the woods could clear itself, suddenly the gladsome light leaped over hill and valley, casting amber, blue, and purple, and a tint of rich red rose …

译文 然而，在树林那流动的景色逝去之前，欢悦的晨光突然跃出了峰峦和山谷，光线所及，把照到的地方和周围的森林分别染成青色、紫色、琥珀色和富丽的红玫瑰色……

解析 "casting"本意是"投、掷"的意思，此处形容光线洒落到不同的地方，森林呈现出不同的色彩，美丽至极。

参考译文

十月的日出

第二天凌晨，在十月的太阳升起之前，我已经起身，穿过了旷野和丛林。十月的清晨乍寒还暖，日出的景象壮观绚丽。透过一片晨曦，朝阳从朦胧的山冈和连绵起伏的高地间，沉重地抬起肩头。在它的逼视下，蒙蒙的雾气下沉，缓缓地散向谷底，接着一丝丝一缕缕地悄悄飘散，笼住峭壁。而在

草地之上悬崖之下的那些隐秘角落里，雾气却还不愿散去，同时群山的雄姿接二连三地显现出来。

森林也层层叠叠地显现，宛若刚刚苏醒的山峦的斗篷，端庄威严，并带着狂风暴雨的回忆。秋天温柔的手已经在抚摸这片山林，因为它们的颜色已经改变，染上了金黄、丹红和橄榄绿。它们对朝日所怀的一片喜悦，像是要奉献给一个新郎，更像是要奉献给一位父亲。

然而，在树林那流动的景色逝去之前，欢悦的晨光突然跃出了峰峦和山谷，光线所及，把照到的地方和周围的森林分别染成青色、紫色、琥珀色和富丽的红玫瑰色。光线照到哪里，哪里就如同一幅幕布被掀开。所有的一切驱散了恐惧和黑暗中的邪恶，所有的一切都插上希望之翼，开始前进，并大声宣告："上帝在这里！"于是生命和欢乐从每一个蜷伏的洞穴里信心十足地欣然跃出；一切花朵、蓓蕾和鸟雀都感受到了生命和欢乐而抖动起来；上帝的凝视汇合成温柔的恩泽。

也许，那永恒的晨光就会这样降临人间，那时不再有险崖沟壑，不再有峰峦山谷，也不再有浩瀚无际的海洋；那时荣耀不会吓走幸福，幸福也不会忌妒荣耀；万物都将踊跃升腾，在造物主慈爱的光芒中生辉，因为太阳已经升起。

读后写作

Seasons may appear different at times. Can you describe the most beautiful season in your life?

Born to Win
生而为赢
——Horatio Alger

读前导语

本篇文章作者霍拉肖·阿尔杰（1832—1899），美国作家，其作品多为鼓舞人心的历险小说。

他在文中写道："人皆生而为新，为前所未有之存在；人皆生而能赢。人皆有其特立独行之方式去审视、聆听、触摸、品味及思考，因而都具备独特潜质——能力和局限。人皆能举足轻重，思虑明达，洞察秋毫，富有创意，成就功业。"

美文欣赏

Each human being is born as something new, something that never existed before. Each is born with the capacity① to win at life. Each person has a unique② way of seeing, hearing, touching, tasting and thinking. Each has his or her own unique potentials—capabilities and limitations. Each can be a significant, thinking, aware, and creative being—a productive person, a winner.

The word "winner" and "loser" have many meanings. When we refer to a person as a winner, we do not mean one who makes someone else lose. To us, a winner is one who responds authentically③ by being credible④, trustworthy, responsive⑤, and genuine, both as an individual and as a member of a society.

Winners do not dedicate their lives to a concept of what they imagine they should be; rather, they are themselves and as such do not use their energy putting on a performance, maintaining pretence and manipulating⑥ others. They are aware that there is a difference between being loving and acting loving, between being stupid and acting stupid, between being knowledgeable and acting knowledgeable. Winners do not need to hide behind a mask.

Winners are not afraid to do their own thinking and to use their own knowledge. They can separate facts from opinions and don't pretend to have all the answers. They listen to others, evaluate what they say, but come to their own conclusions. Although winners can admire and respect other people, they are not totally defined, demolished⑦, bound, or awed by them.

Winners do not play "helpless", nor do they play the blaming game. Instead, they assume responsibility for their own lives. They don't give others a false authority over them. Winners are their own bosses and know it.

A winner's timing is right. Winners respond appropriately⑧ to the situation. Their responses are related to the message sent and preserve⑨ the significance, worth, well-being, and dignity⑩ of the people involved. Winners know that for everything there is a season and for every activity a time.

Although winners can freely enjoy themselves, they can also postpone enjoyment, can discipline⑪ themselves in the present to enhance their enjoyment in the future. Winners are not afraid to go after what they want, but they do so in proper ways. Winners do not get their security by controlling others. They do not set themselves up to lose.

A winner cares about the world and its peoples. A winner is not isolated from the general problems of society, but is concerned, compassionate, and committed to improving the quality of life. Even in the face of national and international adversity⑫, a winner's self-image is not one of a powerless individual. A winner works to make the world a better place.

词汇释义

①**capacity** [kəˈpæsəti] *n.* 能力，才能

②**unique** [juːˈniːk] *adj.* 唯一的；独特的；特有的

③**authentically** [ɔːˈθentɪkli] *adv.* 确实地，真正地

④**credible** [ˈkredəbl] *adj.* 可信的，可靠的；有望成功的

⑤**responsive** [rɪˈspɒnsɪv] *adj.* 应答的，响应的；共鸣的

⑥**manipulate** [məˈnɪpjuleɪt] *vt.* 操作，处理；巧妙地控制；操纵

⑦**demolish** [dɪˈmɒlɪʃ] *v.* 摧毁；推翻；拆毁（尤指大建筑物）

⑧**appropriately** [əˈprəʊpriətli] *adv.* 适当地

⑨**preserve** [prɪˈzɜːv] *v.* 保持；保护；保险；腌制

⑩**dignity** [ˈdɪɡnəti] *n.* 庄严；高贵；尊严；自尊

⑪**discipline** [ˈdɪsəplɪn] *n.* 训练；行为准则 *v.* 训练；惩罚

⑫**adversity** [ədˈvɜːsəti] *n.* 困境，逆境

难句解析

1. To us, a winner is one who responds authentically by being credible, trustworthy, responsive, and genuine, both as an individual and as a member of a society.

译文 对我们而言，成者必为人守信，值得信赖，有求必应，态度诚恳，或为个人，或为社会一员皆能以真诚回应他人。

解析 "a winner is one who responds authentically" 中的 "who responds authentically" 是 "one" 的定语，译为 "真诚地回应"。本句中的 being credible, trustworthy, responsive, and genuine 几个形容词的使用非常精彩。

2. A winner cares about the world and its peoples. A winner is not isolated from the general problems of society, but is concerned, compassionate, and committed to improving the quality of life.

[译文] 成者心忧天下，并不孤立尘世弊病之外，而是置身事内，满腔热情，致力于改善民生。

[解析] "is not isolated from"译为"孤立，脱离"，"is concerned, compassionate, and committed to…"译为"置身事内，满腔热情，致力于……"，与"is not isolated from"形成呼应，再次说明一个成功者应该具有怎样的品质。

参考译文

生而为赢

人皆生而为新，为前所未有之存在；人皆生而能赢。人皆有其特立独行之方式去审视、聆听、触摸、品味及思考，因而都具备独特潜质——能力和局限。人皆能举足轻重，思虑明达，洞察秋毫，富有创意，成就功业。

"成者"与"败者"含义颇多。谈及成者我们并非指令他人失意之人。对我们而言，成者必为人守信，值得信赖，有求必应，态度诚恳，或为个人，或为社会一员皆能以真诚回应他人。

成者行事并不拘泥于某种信条，即便是他们认为应为其奉献一生的理念；而是本色行事，所以并不把精力用来表演，保持伪装或操控他人。他们明了爱与装假，愚蠢与装傻，博学与卖弄之间迥然有别。成者无须藏于面具之后。

成者敢于利用所学，独立思考，区分事实与观点，且并不佯装通晓所有答案。他们倾听、权衡他人意见，但能得出自己的结论。尽管他们尊重、敬佩他人，但并不为他们所局限，所推翻，所束缚，也不对他人敬若神灵。

成者既不佯装"无助"，亦不抱怨他人。相反，他们对人生总是独担责任，也不以权威姿态凌驾他人之上。他们主宰自己，而且能意识到这点。

成者善于审时度势，随机应变。他们对所接收的信息做出回应，维护当事人的利益、康乐和尊严。成者深知成一事要看好时节，行一事要把握时机。

尽管成者可以自由享乐，但他们更知如何推迟享乐，适时自律，以期将来乐趣更盛。成者并不忌惮追求所想，但取之有道，也并不靠控制他人而获取安然之感。他们总是使自己立于不败之地。

成者心忧天下，并不孤立尘世弊病之外，而是置身事内，满腔热情，致力于改善民生。即使面对民族、国家之危亡，成者亦非无力回天之个体。他总是努力令世界变得更好。

读后写作

Different people may have various attitudes towards success. What is your attitude towards success?

The Road to Success
成功之道
——Andrew Carnegie

读前导语

本篇文章作者安德鲁·卡耐基（1835—1919），是苏格兰裔美国实业家、慈善家，卡耐基钢铁公司创始人，被誉为"钢铁大王"和"美国慈善事业之父"。

他在文中写道："成功的首要条件和最大秘诀就是：把你的精力、思想和资本全都集中在你正从事的事业上。一旦开始从事某种职业，就要下定决心在那一领域闯出一片天地来。"

美文欣赏

It is well that young men should begin at the beginning and occupy the most subordinate① positions. Many of the leading businessmen of Pittsburgh had a serious responsibility thrust upon them at the very threshold② of their career. They were introduced to the broom, and spent the first hours of their business lives sweeping out the office. I notice we have janitors③ and janitresses now in offices, and our young men unfortunately miss that salutary④ branch of business education. But if by chance the professional sweeper is absent any morning, the boy who has the genius of the future partner in him will not hesitate to try his hand at the broom⑤. It does not hurt the newest comer to sweep out the office if necessary. I was one of those sweepers myself.

Assuming that you have all obtained employment and are fairly started, my advice to you is "aim high". I would not give a fig for the young man who does not already see himself the partner or the head of an important firm. Do not rest content for a moment in your thoughts as head clerk, or foreman, or general manager in any concern, no matter how extensive⑥. Say to yourself, "My place is at the top." Be king in your dreams.

And here is the prime condition of success, the great secret: concentrate your energy, thought, and capital exclusively upon the business in which you are engaged. Having begun in one line, resolve⑦ to fight it out on that line, to lead in it, adopt every improvement, have the best machinery, and know the most about it.

The concerns which fail are those which have scattered⑧ their capital, which means that they have scattered their brains also. They have investments in this, or that, or the other, here, there, and everywhere. "Don't put all your eggs in one basket" is all wrong. I tell you to "put all your eggs in one basket, and then watch that basket." Look round you and take notice, men who do that not often fail. It is easy to watch and carry the one basket. It is trying to carry too many baskets that breaks most eggs in this country. He who carries three baskets must put one on his head, which is apt to tumble and trip him up. One fault of the American businessman is lack of concentration.

To summarize what I have said: aim for the highest; never enter a bar room; do not touch liquor, or if at all only at meals; never speculate⑨; never indorse⑩ beyond your surplus cash fund; make the firm's interest yours; break orders always to save owners; concentrate; put all your eggs in one basket, and watch that basket; expenditure⑪ always within revenue⑫; lastly, be not impatient, for as Emerson says, "no one can cheat you out of ultimate⑬ success but yourselves."

词汇释义

①**subordinate** [sə'bɔːdɪnət] *adj.* 下级的；次要的；附属的

②**threshold** [ˈθreʃhəʊld] *n.* 门槛，入口；开始；阈

③**janitor** [ˈdʒænɪtə] *n.* 看门人；看管房屋的人

④**salutary** [ˈsæljətri] *adj.* 有益的，效果好的

⑤**broom** [bruːm] *n.* 扫帚；金雀花

⑥**extensive** [ɪkˈstensɪv] *adj.* 广阔的；广泛的；大量的

⑦**resolve** [rɪˈzɒlv] *v.* 决定；下定决心

⑧**scatter** [ˈskætə] *v.* 撒，播撒；（使）散开

⑨**speculate** [ˈspekjuleɪt] *v.* 思索，猜测，推测

⑩**indorse** [ɪnˈdɔːs] *v.* 签名于票据等的背面；认可

⑪**expenditure** [ɪkˈspendɪtʃə(r)] *n.* 花费；消耗

⑫**revenue** [ˈrevənjuː] *n.* 税收；财政收入；收益

⑬**ultimate** [ˈʌltɪmət] *adj.* 最后的；极限的；首要的；最好的

难句解析

1. Assuming that you have all obtained employment and are fairly started, my advice to you is "aim high". I would not give a fig for the young man who does not already see himself the partner or the head of an important firm.

译文 假如你们已经被录用，并且有了一个良好的开端，我对你们的建议是：要志存高远。一个年轻人，如果不把自己想象成一家大公司未来的老板或者是合伙人，那我会对他不屑一顾。

解析 "assuming"译为"假如"，后面常用从句来表达假设的内容；"fairly"的本义是"相当地"，此处译为"良好地"；"not give a fig for"译为"不在乎，认为无所谓"，"fig"指的是"无花果"。

2. To summarize what I have said: aim for the highest; never enter a bar room; do not touch liquor, or if at all only at meals; never speculate; never indorse beyond your surplus cash fund; ...

译文 把我的话归纳一下：要志存高远；不要出入酒吧；要滴酒不沾，或要喝也只在用餐时喝少许；不要做投机买卖；不要寅吃卯粮；要把公司的利益当作自己的利益；……

解析 "aim for the highest" 此处译为 "志存高远,有很高的志向";"if at all" 译为 "就算真的有,也……（置于句末,具体意思根据句子前半部分而定）";"never indorse beyond your surplus cash fund" 中的 "indorse" 译为 "签名于票据等的背面,认可",在本句中可以理解为 "全力维护公司的利益"。

参考译文

成功之道

年轻人创业之初,应该从最底层干起,这是件好事。匹兹堡有很多商业巨头,他们在创业之初,都肩负过 "重任"。他们以扫帚为伴,以打扫办公室的方式度过了他们商业生涯中最初的时光。我注意到我们现在办公室里都有工友,于是年轻人就不幸错过了商业教育中这个有益的环节。如果碰巧哪天上午专职扫地的工友没有来,某个具有未来合伙人气质的年轻人会毫不犹豫地试着拿起扫帚。在必要时新来的员工扫扫地也无妨,不会因此而有什么损失。我自己就曾经扫过地。

假如你们已经被录用,并且有了一个良好的开端,我对你们的建议是:要志存高远。一个年轻人,如果不把自己想象成一家大公司未来的老板或者是合伙人,那我会对他不屑一顾。不论职位有多高,你的内心都不要满足于做一个总管、领班或者总经理。要对自己说:"我要迈向顶尖!"要做就做你梦想中的国王!

成功的首要条件和最大秘诀就是:把你的精力、思想和资本全都集中在你正从事的事业上。一旦开始从事某种职业,就要下定决心在那一领域闯出一片天地来,做这一行的领导人物,接纳每一点改进之心,采用最优良的设备,对专业知识熟稔于心。

一些公司的失败就在于他们分散了资金,因为这就意味着分散了他们的精力。他们向这方面投资,又向那方面投资;在这里投资,在那里投资,到处都投资。"不要把所有的鸡蛋放在一个篮子里" 的说法大错特错。我要对你说:"把所有的鸡蛋都放在一个篮子里,然后小心地看好那个篮子。" 看看你周围,你会注意到:这么做的人其实很少失败。看管和携带一个篮子并不太难。人们总是试图提很多篮子，所以才打破这个国家的大部分鸡蛋。提三个篮子的人，必须把一个顶在头上，而这个篮子很可能掉下来，把他自己绊倒。美国商人的一个缺点就是不够专注。

把我的话归纳一下：要志存高远；不要出入酒吧；要滴酒不沾，或要喝也只在用餐时喝少许；不要做投机买卖；不要寅吃卯粮；要把公司的利益当作自己的利益；取消订货的目的永远是为了挽救货主；要专注；要把所有的鸡蛋放在一个篮子里，然后小心地看好它；要量入为出；最后，要有耐心，正如爱默生所言："谁都无法阻止你最终成功，除非你自己承认自己失败。"

读后写作

Please summarize the approaches to success mentioned in the passage. If you have more ways to achieve success, please tell us.

Nature
自 然
——Ralph Waldo Emerson

读前导语

本篇文章作者拉尔夫·沃尔多·爱默生（1803—1882），生于美国波士顿。美国思想家、文学家、诗人。爱默生是确立美国文化精神的代表人物，是新英格兰超验主义最杰出的代言人。美国前总统林肯称他为"美国的孔子""美国文明之父"。代表作品有《论自然》《美国学者》。其中《论自然》被认为是"新英格兰超验主义的圣经"，而《美国学者》被誉为"美国思想文化领域的独立宣言"。

他在文中写道："自然的热爱者，他内心和外在的感觉仍然是协调变化的，即使进入成年，他仍能保有童时的心灵。与天国和尘世的交流成为他每天生活的一部分。"

美文欣赏

To go into solitude①, a man needs to retire as much from his chamber② as from society. I am not solitary③ whilst④ I read and write, though nobody is with me.

But if a man would be alone, let him look at the stars. The rays that come from those heavenly worlds, will separate between him and what he touches. One might think the atmosphere was made transparent⑤ with this design, to give man, in the heavenly bodies, the perpetual⑥ presence of the sublime⑦. Seen in the streets of cities, how great they are!

If the stars should appear one night in a thousand years, how would men believe and adore; and preserve for many generations the remembrance⑧ of the city of God which had been shown! But every night come out these envoys of beauty, and light the universe with their admonishing⑨ smile.

The stars awaken a certain reverence⑩, because though always present, they are inaccessible⑪; but all natural objects make a kindred impression, when the mind is open to their influence. Nature never wears a mean appearance. Neither does the wisest man extort⑫ her secret, and lose his curiosity by finding out all her perfection. Nature never became a toy to a wise spirit. The flowers, the animals, the mountains, reflected the wisdom of his best hour, as much as they had delighted the simplicity⑬ of his childhood.

When we speak of nature in this manner, we have a distinct but most poetical sense in the mind. We mean the integrity of impression made by manifold⑭ natural objects. It is this which distinguishes the stick of timber of the wood-cutter, from the tree of the poet.

The charming landscape which I saw this morning, is indubitably⑮ made up of some twenty or thirty farms. Miller owns this field, Locke that, and Manning the woodland beyond. But none of them owns the landscape. There is a property⑯ in the horizon which no man has but he whose eye can integrate all the parts, that is, the poet. This is the best part of these men's farms, yet to this their warranty-deeds give no title.

To speak truly, few adult persons can see nature. Most persons do not see the sun. At least they have a very superficial⑰ seeing. The sun illuminates⑱ only the eye of the man, but shines into the eye and the heart of the child. The lover of nature is he whose inward and outward senses are still truly adjusted to each other; who has retained the spirit of infancy even into the era of manhood. His intercourse with heaven and earth, becomes part of his daily food.

词汇释义

①**solitude** [ˈsɒlətjuːd] n. 单独；孤独；隐居处；荒野

②**chamber** [ˈtʃeɪmbə(r)] n. 房间；议院；私人房间

③**solitary** ['sɒlətri] *adj.* 独自的，独立的；单个的；唯一的；隐居的

④**whilst** [waɪlst] *conj.* 在……期间；与……同时；然而；尽管

⑤**transparent** [træns'pærənt] *adj.* 透明的；易懂的；易识破的

⑥**perpetual** [pə'petʃuəl] *adj.* 永久的；不断的；无期限的

⑦**sublime** [sə'blaɪm] *n.* 庄严，崇高；至高无上，顶点

⑧**remembrance** [rɪ'membrəns] *n.* 回想，回忆；记忆，记忆力

⑨**admonish** [əd'mɒnɪʃ] *v.* 劝告；训诫；轻责

⑩**reverence** ['revərəns] *n.* 尊敬，敬畏；敬礼；受尊敬；尊严

⑪**inaccessible** [ˌɪnæk'sesəbl] *adj.* 达不到的；不能接近的

⑫**extort** [ɪk'stɔːt] *vt.* 敲诈；强夺

⑬**simplicity** [sɪm'plɪsəti] *n.* 简单，朴素；质朴，天真；愚蠢；无知

⑭**manifold** ['mænɪfəʊld] *adj.* 多方面的；有多种用途的

⑮**indubitably** [ɪn'djuːbɪtəbli] *adv.* 无疑地，确实地

⑯**property** ['prɒpəti] *n.* 财产；房地产；特性；属性

⑰**superficial** [ˌsuːpə'fɪʃl] *adj.* 表面的；肤浅的；缺乏深度的

⑱**illuminate** [ɪ'luːmɪneɪt] *v.* 照亮，照明；阐明，说明；装饰

难句解析

1. To go into solitude, a man needs to retire as much from his chamber as from society. I am not solitary whilst I read and write, though nobody is with me.

译文 人不仅要远离社会，还需远离书房，方可进入孤独的境界。当我读书写作时，虽然无人相伴，但并不孤独。

解析 "go into solitude" 译为 "脱离，远离（社会）"，"retire" 本义是 "退休"，此处可以理解为 "远离"，"chamber" 在此处译为 "私人房间，私人空间"，"whilst" 译为 "在……期间"，作者想表达的意思是 "他虽然独自一人，但从未感到孤单"。

2. The stars awaken a certain reverence, because though always present, they are inaccessible; but all natural objects make a kindred impression, when the mind is open

to their influence.

[译文] 繁星虽然每晚都会出现，人类却无法接近，也因而对其心生敬畏之情。当你放开心灵去感受万物时，你会发现一切自然之物都像星辰那样，令人产生类似的感觉。

[解析] "awaken"译为"唤醒，（使）觉醒；（使）意识到"，"reverence"译为"尊敬，敬畏"，"awaken a certain reverence"译为"唤起某种敬畏之情"；"is open to"译为"敞开心扉，愿意接受"。

参考译文

自　然

人不仅要远离社会，还需远离书房，方可进入孤独的境界。当我读书写作时，虽然无人相伴，但并不孤独。

仰望星空吧，它会让人体验到什么是孤独。来自天国的光芒将你和你所接触的世界分离。你或许会想到，空气之所以是透明的，就是要让人类感受到天体那亘古不变的崇高和壮美。在城市的街道上仰望它们，多么壮观啊！

假如这些繁星在一千年中仅仅出现一次，人们将如何信仰和崇拜它们啊，又将如何代代相传，纪念那上帝之城的光芒啊！然而，每一晚，这些美的使者都以训诫的微笑照亮寰宇。

繁星虽然每晚都会出现，人类却无法接近，也因而对其心生敬畏之情。当你放开心灵去感受万物时，你会发现一切自然之物都像星辰那样，令人产生类似的感觉。大自然从不平凡。最聪明的智者也无法穷尽自然的秘密，不会因发现自然的完美而失去好奇心。对智者来说，自然绝不是一个玩物。鲜花、动物、山峦愉悦了他纯真的童年，也映射出他睿智的盛年。

当我们这样描述自然时，我们的感觉是清晰又极具诗意的。我们指的是各种自然物给予人的整体印象。正是这种整体印象将伐木工人看到的木头与诗人眼中的树木区别开来。

今天早上我看到的迷人景象是由二三十个农场构成的。这块地属于米勒，旁边那块是洛克的，再远处的山林是曼宁的。然而，这迷人的风景却不属于他们中的任何一位。只有诗人的眼睛才能将一个个农场的美景凝为一体。农场的景色融为一体才最美，这并非农场主人的地契所能赋予的。

坦白地说，没有几个成年人能发现自然。大多数人意识不到太阳的存在。至少，他们对自然的理解是非常肤浅的。阳光仅能帮助成年人视物，却能深入孩童的眼睛和心灵。自然的热爱者，他内心和外在的感觉仍然是协调变化的，即使进入成年，他仍能保有童时的心灵。与天国和尘世的交流成为他每天生活的一部分。

读后写作

With the rapid pace of urban life, we seldom have time to get close to nature. Please introduce an experience when you get close to nature.

How to Read a Good Book
怎样读一本好书
——John Ruskin

读前导语

本篇文章作者约翰·罗斯金（1819—1900），英国作家和美术评论家，他对社会的评论使他被视为道德领路人或预言家。

他在书中写道："在书的世界里，你可以任意驰骋。你可以结识许多伟大的人物，建立起高贵的友谊，在与这些伟人的交往中，你会进一步认识自己的思想格调，提高自己的道德修养，以你所崇拜的人物来衡量自己的行为，激励自己在社会生活中不断追求更高尚的目标。"

美文欣赏

First, by a true desire to be taught by them, and to enter into their thoughts. To enter into theirs, observe; not to find your own expressed by them. If the person who wrote the book is not wiser than you, you need not read it; if he be, he will think differently from you in many respects.

Very ready we are to say of a book, "How good this is—that's exactly what I think!" But the right feeling is, "How strange that is! I never thought of that before, and yet I see it is true; or if I do not now, I hope I shall, some day." But whether thus submissively[①] or not, at least be sure that you go to the author to get at his meaning, not to find yours. Judge it afterwards if you think yourself qualified[②] to do so; but ascertain[③] it first. And be sure also, if the author is worth anything, that you will not get at his meaning all at once; — nay, that at his whole meaning you will not for a long time arrive in any wise. Not that he does not say what he means, and in strong words too; but he cannot say it all; and what is more strange, will not, but in a hidden way and in parables④, in order that he may be sure you want it. I cannot quite see the reason of this, nor analyse⑤ that cruel reticence⑥ in the breasts of wise men which makes them always hide their deeper thought. They do not give it to you by way of help, but of reward; and will make themselves sure that you deserve it before they allow you to reach it. But it is the same with the physical type of wisdom, gold. There seems, to you and me, no reason why the electric forces of the earth should not carry whatever there is of gold within it at once to the mountain tops, so that kings and people might know that all the gold they could get was there; and without any trouble of digging⑦, or anxiety, or chance, or waste of time, cut it away, and coin as much as they needed. But Nature does not manage it so. She puts it in little fissures⑧ in the earth, nobody knows where: you may dig long and find none; you must dig painfully to find any.

词汇释义

①**submissively** [səbˈmɪsɪvli] *adv.* 顺从地，服从地
②**qualified** [ˈkwɒlɪfaɪd] *adj.* 有资格的；具备……学历/资历的
③**ascertain** [ˌæsəˈteɪn] *v.* 查明，弄清；确定
④**parable** [ˈpærəbl] *n.* （圣经中的）寓言故事
⑤**analyse** [ˈænəlaɪz] *v.* 分析；分解；化验
⑥**reticence** [ˈretɪsns] *n.* 不轻易暴露想法或感情；沉默；含蓄
⑦**dig** [dɪɡ] *v.* 挖，掘，戳，掏；寻找，搜寻；喜欢
⑧**fissure** [ˈfɪʃə(r)] *n.* 狭长裂缝或裂隙；裂伤；分歧；分裂

难句解析

1. If the person who wrote the book is not wiser than you, you need not read it; if he be, he will think differently from you in many respects.

译文 如果书的作者不比你睿智，就不必读他的书；如果他比你睿智，他会在许多方面和你的想法不同。

解析 "if he be" 可理解为 "if he is wiser than you"; "think differently" 译

为"想得不一样";"in many respects"译为"在很多方面",本句作者想表达的意思是"让我们时刻保持清醒,善于读书,善于从别人的书中学习到各种知识"。

2. There seems, to you and me, no reason why the electric forces of the earth should not carry whatever there is of gold within it at once to the mountain tops, so that kings and people might know that all the gold they could get was there...

[译文] 在你我看来,似乎毫无道理,地球的电磁力为什么不把富含黄金的东西统统搬到山顶上去,这样国王们和芸芸众生就会知道他们能弄到手的黄金都在那里……

[解析] "There seems, to you and me, no reason why..."中的"to you and me"为插入语,主干部分"There seems no reason why..."译为"似乎毫无道理……";"so that..."译为"因此,所以"。

参考译文

怎样读一本好书

首先,要怀着真诚的愿望向作者学习,融入他们的思想中。要融入他们的思想,细心观察,而不是找出他们表达的和你一样的思想观念。如果书的作者不比你睿智,就不必读他的书;如果他比你睿智,他会在许多方面和你的想法不同。

我们老这样说一本书:"写得多好哇——正是我所想的!"但是正确的感受是:"多奇怪呀!我以前从没想到过,但我明白这是真知灼见;要是我现在不明白的话,我希望自己有一天会明白。"但不论是否如此恭顺,至少一定要走近作者,去理解他的意思,而不是找你的想法。读后进行分析判断,如果你认为自己够格的话;但首先要弄清作者的意思。还要知道,如果作者有点真东西的话,你不可能一下子把他的意思全部弄懂;——不,对于他的全部见解,你无论如何要等很长时间才能懂得。并不是因为他言不及义,没有说清楚;而是因为他不能全部说出;更离奇的是,他不愿全部说出,而是说得含蓄,用寓言去说,意在他能肯定你需要它。我不大能明白其中的缘由,也分析不了这些睿智的人胸中无情的缄默,总是使他们把自己更深刻的思想藏而不露。他们不是以帮助的方式把思想显露在你面前,而是以奖赏的方式;他们要使自己确信你配得上他们的思想,才允许你接触到。而这种情况与智慧的物质形态黄金类似。在你我看来，似乎毫无道理，地球的电磁力为什么不把富含黄金的东西统统搬到山顶上去，这样国王们和芸芸众生就会知道他们能弄到手的黄金都在那里，不用辛辛苦苦去挖掘，不用忧心、碰运气，也不用浪费时间，一挖就走，想造多少金币就造多少金币。但是大自然不是这么安排的。她把黄金放在地球的隙缝里，无人知晓在何处；你可能长时间地挖呀挖而一无所获；你必须不辞辛劳地挖才能找到一点点。

读后写作

As is written in the passage, books are the most faithful friends to us. Please summarize the ways to read books in the passage.

Human Life Like a Poem
人生如诗
——Lin Yutang

读前导语

本篇文章作者林语堂（1895—1976），中国现代著名作家、学者、翻译家、语言学家。

他在文中写道："我以为，从生物学角度看，人的一生恰如诗歌。人生自有其韵律和节奏，自有内在的生成与衰亡。人生始于无邪的童年，经过少年的青涩，带着激情与无知、理想与雄心，笨拙而努力地走向成熟。"

美文欣赏

I think that, from a biological standpoint[①], human life almost reads like a poem. It has its own rhythm and beat, its internal[②] cycles of growth and decay. It begins with innocent[③] childhood, followed by awkward[④] adolescence trying awkwardly to adapt itself to mature society, with its young passions and follies[⑤], its ideals and ambitions; then it reaches a manhood of intense activities, profiting[⑥] from experience and learning more about society and human nature; at middle age, there is a slight easing of tension, a mellowing of character like the ripening of fruit or the mellowing[⑦] of good wine, and the gradual acquiring of a more tolerant, more cynical and at the same time a kindlier view of life; then in the sunset of our life, the endocrine[⑧] glands decrease their activity, and if we have a true philosophy of old age and have ordered our life pattern according to it, it is for us the age of peace and security and leisure and contentment; finally, life flickers out and one goes into eternal sleep, never to wake up again.

One should be able to sense the beauty of this rhythm of life, to appreciate, as we do in grand symphonies⑨, its main theme, its strains of conflict and the final resolution⑩. The movements of these cycles are very much the same in a normal life, but the music must be provided by the individual himself. In some souls, the discordant⑪ note becomes harsher and harsher and finally overwhelms or submerges the main melody. Sometimes the discordant note gains so much power that the music can no longer go on, and the individual shoots himself with a pistol or jump into a river. But that is because his original leitmotif⑫ has been hopelessly over-showed through the lack of a good self-education. Otherwise the normal human life runs to its normal end in kind of dignified movement and procession. There are sometimes in many of us too many staccatos⑬ or impetuosos, and because the tempo⑭ is wrong, the music is not pleasing to the ear; we might have more of the grand rhythm and majestic tempo of the Ganges, flowing slowly and eternally into the sea.

No one can say that life with childhood, manhood and old age is not a beautiful arrangement; the day has its morning, noon and sunset, and the year has its seasons, and it is good that it is so. There is no good or bad in life, except what is good according to its own season. And if we take this biological view of life and try to live according to the seasons, no one but a conceited⑮ fool or an impossible idealist can deny that human life can be lived like a poem. Shakespeare has expressed this idea more graphically in his passage about the seven stages of life, and a good many Chinese writers have said about the same thing. It is curious that Shakespeare was never very religious, or very much concerned with religion. I think this was his greatness; he took human life largely as it was, and intruded⑯ himself as little upon the general scheme of things as he did upon the characters of his plays. Shakespeare was like Nature itself, and that is the greatest compliment⑰ we can pay to a writer or thinker. He merely lived, observed life and went away.

词汇释义

①**standpoint** [ˈstændpɔɪnt] *n.* 立场，观点

②**internal** [ɪnˈtɜːnl] *adj.* 内部的；体内的；国内的；内心的

③**innocent** [ˈɪnəsnt] *adj.* 无辜的；天真无邪的；无知的

④**awkward** [ˈɔːkwəd] *adj.* 使人尴尬的；棘手的；难使用的

⑤**folly** [ˈfɒli] *n.* 蠢笨；愚行；讽刺剧

⑥**profit** [ˈprɒfɪt] *v.* 获益；得益于 *n.* 利润；好处

⑦**mellowing** [ˈmeləʊɪŋ] *n.* 软化，醇化

⑧**endocrine** [ˈendəʊkrɪn] *adj.* 内分泌（腺）的，激素的

⑨**symphony** [ˈsɪmfəni] *n.* 交响乐，交响曲

⑩**resolution** [ˌrezəˈluːʃn] *n.* 决心；解决；坚决

⑪**discordant** [dɪsˈkɔːdənt] *adj.* 不和的；不一致的；不调和的

⑫**leitmotif** [ˈlaɪtməʊtiːf] *n.* 主乐调，主旨

⑬**staccato** [stəˈkɑːtəʊ] *n.* 断奏的曲乐段，断唱

⑭**tempo** [ˈtempəʊ] *n.* [乐] 速度，拍子；（运动或活动的）速度

⑮**conceited** [kənˈsiːtɪd] *adj.* 自负的，傲慢的

⑯**intrude** [ɪnˈtruːd] *v.* 侵入，侵扰，打扰；闯入

⑰**compliment** [ˈkɒmplɪmənt] *n.* 赞美，恭维；致意；祝贺

难句解析

1. It begins with innocent childhood, followed by awkward adolescence trying awkwardly to adapt itself to mature society, with its young passions and follies, its ideals and ambitions;…

译文 人生始于无邪的童年，经过少年的青涩，带着激情与无知、理想与雄心，笨拙而努力地走向成熟；……

解析 "innocent childhood" 和 "awkward adolescence" 分别写出了童年时期的天真无邪和少年时期的青涩，能使读者深刻地体会到自己走过的人生之路，与 "mature society" 形成对比，再和每个时期的 "its young passions and follies, its ideals and ambitions" 结合起来，生动而又形象。

2. I think this was his greatness; he took human life largely as it was, and intruded himself as little upon the general scheme of things as he did upon the characters of his plays.

译文 我想这正是他的伟大之处，他对人生秉着顺其自然的态度，他对生活之事的干涉和改动很少，正如他对戏剧人物那样。

[解析] "took human life largely as"和"intruded himself as little upon the general scheme of things as"之中的"largely"和"little"形成对比，表达出人生之大和我们自己的渺小。

3. It is curious that Shakespeare was never very religious, or very much concerned with religion.

[译文] 奇怪的是，莎士比亚并不是虔诚的宗教徒，也不怎么关心宗教。

[解析] "It is curious that..."是主语从句；"be concerned with"译为"关心"。

参考译文

人生如诗

我以为，从生物学角度看，人的一生恰如诗歌。人生自有其韵律和节奏，自有内在的生成与衰亡。人生始于无邪的童年，经过少年的青涩，带着激情与无知、理想与雄心，笨拙而努力地走向成熟；后来人到壮年，经历渐广，阅人渐多，涉世渐深，收益也渐大；及至中年，人生的紧张得以舒缓，人的性格日渐成熟，如芳馥之果实，如醇美之佳酿，更具容忍之心，处世虽更悲观，但对人生的态度趋于和善；再后来就是人生迟暮，内分泌系统活动减少，若此时吾辈已经悟得老年真谛，并据此安排残年，那生活将和平而宁静，安详而知足；终于，生命之烛摇曳而终熄灭，人开始永恒地长眠，不再醒来。

人们当学会感受生命韵律之美，像听交响乐一样，欣赏其主旋律、激昂的高潮和舒缓的尾声。这些反复的乐章对于我们的生命都大同小异，但个人的乐曲却要自己去谱写。在某些人心中，不和谐音会越来越刺耳，最终竟然能掩盖主曲；有时不和谐音会积蓄巨大的能量，令乐曲不能继续，这时人们或举枪自杀或投河自尽。这是他最初的主题被无望地遮蔽，只因他缺少自我教育。否则，常人将以体面的运动和进程走向既定的终点。在我们多数人胸中常常会有太多的断奏或强音，那是因为节奏错了，生命的乐曲因此而不再悦耳。我们应该如恒河，学她气势恢宏而豪迈地缓缓流向大海。

人生有童年、少年和老年，谁也不能否认这是一种美好的安排，一天要有清晨、正午和日落，一年要有四季之分，如此才好。人生本无好坏之分，只是各个季节有各自的好处。如若我们持此种生物学的观点，并循着季节去生活，除了狂妄自大的傻瓜和无可救药的理想主义者，谁能说人生不能像诗一般度过呢？莎翁在他的一段话中形象地阐述了人生分七个阶段的观点，很多中国作家也说过类似的话。奇怪的是，莎士比亚并不是虔诚的宗教徒，也不怎么关心宗教。我想这正是他的伟大之处，他对人生秉着顺其自然的态度，他对生活之事的干涉和改动很少，正如他对戏剧人物那样。莎翁就像自然一样，这是我们能给作家或思想家的最高褒奖。对人生，他只是一路经历着，观察着，离我们远去了。

读后写作

As is written in the passage, life is like a poem. Do you agree with it? Express your own opinion.

Beautiful Smile and Love
美丽的微笑与爱心
——Mother Teresa

读前导语

本篇文章作者特蕾莎修女（1910—1997），印度著名的慈善家，印度天主教仁爱传教会创始人，在世界范围内建立了一个庞大的慈善机构网，赢得了国际社会的广泛尊敬。1979年被授予诺贝尔和平奖。本文所选即她在领取该奖项时的演讲词，语言简洁质朴而感人至深。诺贝尔奖领奖台上响起的声音往往都文采飞扬、热烈、激昂，而特雷莎修女的演说朴实无华，其所举事例听来似平凡之至，然而其中所蕴含的伟大而神圣的爱感人至深。平凡中孕育伟大，真情才能动人。

她在文中写道："因此，让我们总是微笑相见，因为微笑就是爱的开端，一旦我们开始彼此自然地相爱，我们就会想着为对方做点什么了。"

美文欣赏

The poor are very wonderful people. One evening we went out and we picked up four people from the street. And one of them was in a most terrible condition, and I told the sisters: You take care of the other three. I take care of this one who looked worse. So I did for her all that my love can do. I put her in bed, and there was such a beautiful smile on her face. She took hold of my hand as she said just the words "thank you" and she died. I could not help but examine my conscience[①] before her and I asked what would I say if I was in her place. And my answer was very simple. I would have tried to draw a little attention to myself. I would have said I am hungry, that I am dying, I am cold, I am in pain, or something, but she gave me much more—she gave me her grateful② love. And she died with a smile on her face. As did that man whom we picked up from the drain, half-eaten with worms③, and we brought him to the home. "I have lived like an animal in the street, but I am going to die like an angel, loved and cared for." And it was so wonderful to see the greatness of that man who could speak like that, who could die like that without blaming④ anybody, without cursing⑤ anybody, without comparing anything. Like an angel—this is the greatness of our people. And that is why we believe what Jesus had said: I was hungry, I was naked⑥, I was homeless, I was unwanted, unloved, uncared for, and you did it to me.

I believe that we are not real social workers. We may be doing social work in the eyes of the people, but we are really contemplatives⑦ in the heart of the world. For we are touching the body of Christ twenty-four hours... And I think that in our family we don't need bombs and guns, to destroy, to bring peace, just get together, love one another, bring that peace, that joy, that strength of presence of each other in the home. And we will be able to overcome all the evil that is in the world.

And with this prize that I have received as a Prize of Peace, I am going to try to make the home for many people who have no home. Because I believe that love begins at home, and if we can create a home for the poor, I think that more and more love will spread. And we will be able through this understanding love to bring peace to the poor. The poor in our own family first, then in our country and in the world. To be able to do this, our Sisters, our lives have to be woven with prayer⑧. They have to be woven with Christ to be able to understand, to be able to share. Because to be woven⑨ with Christ is to be able to understand, to be able to share. Because today there is so much suffering... When I pick up a person from the street, hungry, I give him a plate of rice, a piece of bread. I have satisfied. I have removed that hunger. But a person who is shut out, who feels unwanted, unloved, terrified, the person who has been thrown out from society—that poverty is so full of hurt and so unbearable... And so let us always meet each other with a smile, for the smile is the beginning of love, and once we begin to love each other naturally we want to do something.

词汇释义

①**conscience** [ˈkɒnʃəns] *n.* 良心，良知；内疚

②**grateful** [ˈgreɪtfl] *adj.* 感激的；表示感谢的

③**worm** [wɜːm] *n.* 蠕虫；（动物或人体内）寄生虫

④**blame** [bleɪm] *v.* 责怪，指责

⑤**curse** [kɜːs] *v.* 诅咒，咒骂

⑥**naked** [ˈneɪkɪd] *adj.* 裸露的；率直的；赤裸裸的；缺乏保护的

⑦**contemplative** [kənˈtemplətɪv] *adj.* 沉思的，冥思的 *n.* 沉思默想的人；敛心默祷者

⑧**prayer** [preə(r)] *n.* 祈祷；祷词；祈望；祈祷仪式

⑨**woven** [ˈwəʊvn] （weave 的过去分词）*v.* 编，织；编排；杜撰

难句解析

1. I could not help but examine my conscience before her and I asked what would I say if I was in her place.

译文 我情不自禁地在她面前审视起自己的良知来。我问自己，如果我是她的话，会说些什么呢？

解析 "I could not help but examine" 的结构为 "I could not help but do sth."，译为 "情不自禁做某事"；"in her place" 译为 "在她的位置上"。

2. And so let us always meet each other with a smile, for the smile is the beginning of love, and once we begin to love each other naturally we want to do something.

译文 因此，让我们总是微笑相见，因为微笑就是爱的开端，一旦我们开始彼此自然地相爱，我们就会想着为对方做点什么了。

解析 "for" 译为 "因为"； "once we begin to love each other naturally we want to do something" 中的 "once" 译为 "一旦"，此处引导条件状语从句。

参考译文

美丽的微笑与爱心

穷人是非常了不起的人。一天晚上，我们外出，从街上带回了四个人，其中一个生命岌岌可危。于是我告诉修女们说："你们照料其他三个，这个濒危的人就由我来照顾。"就这样，我为她做了我的爱所能做的一切。我将她放在床上，看到她的脸上绽露出如此美丽的微笑。她握着我的手，只说了

句"谢谢您"就死了。我情不自禁地在她面前审视起自己的良知来。我问自己，如果我是她的话，会说些什么呢？答案很简单，我会尽量引起旁人对我的关注，我会说我饥饿难忍，奄奄一息，冷得发抖，痛苦不堪，诸如此类的话。但是她给我的却更多更多——她给了我她的感激之情。她死时脸上却带着微笑。我们从排水道带回的那个男子也是如此。当时，他几乎全身都快被虫子吃掉了，我们把他带回了家。"在街上，我一直像个动物一样地活着，但我将像个天使一样地死去，有人爱，有人关心。"真是太好了，我看到了他的伟大之处，他竟能说出那样的话。他那样地死去，不责怪任何人，不诅咒任何人，无欲无求。像天使一样——这便是我们的人民的伟大之所在。因此我们相信耶稣所说的话：我饥肠辘辘，我衣不蔽体，我无家可归，我不为人所要，不为人所爱，也不为人所关心，然而，你却为我做了这一切。

  我想，我们算不上真正的社会工作者。在人们的眼中，或许我们是在做社会工作，但实际上，我们真的只是世界中心的修行者。因为，一天24小时，我们都在触摸基督的圣体。我想，在我们的大家庭里，我们不需要枪支和炮弹来破坏和平，或带来和平——我们只需要团结起来，彼此相爱，将和平、欢乐以及每一个家庭成员灵魂的活力都带回世界。这样，我们就能战胜世界上现存的一切邪恶。

  我准备以我所获得的诺贝尔和平奖奖金为那些无家可归的人们建立自己的家园。因为我相信，爱源自家庭，如果我们能为穷人建立家园，我想爱便会传播得更广。而且，我们将通过这种宽容博大的爱而带来和平，成为穷人的福音。首先为我们自己家里的穷人，其次为我们国家，为全世界的穷人。为了做到这一点，姐妹们，我们的生活就必须与祷告紧紧相连，必须同基督结合一体才能互相体谅，共同分享，因为同基督结合一体就意味着互相体谅，共同分享。因为，今天的世界上仍有如此多的苦难存在……当我从街上带回一个饥肠辘辘的人时，给他一盘饭，一片面包，我就能使他心满意足了，我就能驱除他的饥饿。但是，如果一个人露宿街头，感到不为人所要，不为人所爱，惶恐不安，被社会抛弃——这样的贫困让人心痛，如此令人无法忍受……因此，让我们总是微笑相见，因为微笑就是爱的开端，一旦我们开始彼此自然地相爱，我们就会想着为对方做点什么了。

读后写作

　　A smile is a beautiful flower that blooms on people's faces, exuding a charming fragrance all the time. Smiling is an international language. A smile is only a moment, but the memories it leaves behind live on. Have you ever met any person whose smiling face is very impressive? Please share the story with us.

Mirror, Mirror—What do I See?
镜子，镜子，告诉我
——Derek Walcott

读前导语

本篇文章作者德里克·沃尔科特（1930—2017），生于圣卢西亚的卡斯特里。先后就读于圣玛利大学和西印度的牙买加大学，毕业后迁居特立尼达岛。在波士顿大学教授过文学课程。诗人、剧作家及画家，代表作有《奥美罗斯》《白鹭》等。国际作家奖、史密斯文学奖、麦克阿瑟奖、艾略特诗歌奖等的获得者。1992年，其诗因"具有伟大的光彩，历史的视野，献身多元文化的结果"，获诺贝尔文学奖。他被布罗茨基誉为"今日英语文学中最好的诗人"。

他在文中写道："充满爱意的人生活在充满爱意的世界里，充满敌意的人则生活在充满敌意的世界里。你所遇到的每一个人都是你的镜子。"

美文欣赏

A loving person lives in a loving world. A hostile[①] person lives in a hostile world. Everyone you meet is your mirror.

Mirrors have a very particular function. They reflect[②] the image in front of them. Just as a physical mirror serves as the vehicle[③] to reflection, so do all of the people in our lives.

When we see something beautiful such as a flower garden, that garden serves as a reflection. In order to see the beauty in front of us, we must be able to see the beauty inside of ourselves. When we love someone, it's a reflection of loving ourselves. We have often heard things like "I love how I am when I'm with that person." That simply translates into "I'm able to love me when I love that other person." Oftentimes, when we meet someone new, we feel as though we "click". Sometimes it's as if we've known each other for a long time. That feeling can come from sharing similarities.

Just as the "mirror" or other person can be a positive reflection, it is more likely that we'll notice it when it has a negative connotation④. For example, it's easy to remember times when we have met someone we're not particularly crazy about. We may have some criticism⑤ in our mind about the person. This is especially true when we get to know someone with whom we would rather spend less time.

Frequently⑥, when we dislike qualities in other people, ironically⑦, it's usually the mirror that's speaking to us.

I began questioning myself further each time I encountered⑧ someone that I didn't particularly like. Each time, I asked myself, "What is it about that person that I don't like?" and then "Is there something similar in me?" In every instance, I could see a piece of that quality in me, and sometimes I had to really get very introspective⑨. So what did that mean?

It means that just as I can get annoyed⑩ or disturbed when I notice that aspect in someone else, I better reexamine my qualities and consider making some changes. Even if I'm not willing to make a drastic⑪ change, at least I consider how I might modify⑫ some of the things that I'm doing.

At times we meet someone new and feel distant, disconnected, or disgusted. Although we don't want to believe it, and it's not easy or desirable to look further, it can be a great learning lesson to figure out what part of the person is being reflected in you. It's simply just another way to create more self-awareness.

词汇释义

①**hostile** [ˈhɒstaɪl] *adj.* 敌人的，敌对的；怀有敌意的；不利的

②**reflect** [rɪˈflekt] *v.* 照出（影像）；反映；反射；沉思；表达

③**vehicle** [ˈviːəkl] *n.* 车辆，交通工具；手段，工具

④**connotation** [ˌkɒnəˈteɪʃn] *n.* 含义；隐含意义

⑤**criticism** [ˈkrɪtɪsɪzəm] *n.* 批判；指责；（书籍或音乐等）评论

⑥**frequently** [ˈfriːkwəntli] *adv.* 频繁地，经常

⑦**ironically** [aɪˈrɒnɪkli] *adv.* 嘲讽地，挖苦地；具有讽刺意味地
⑧**encounter** [ɪnˈkaʊntə(r)] *v.* 遭遇；偶遇
⑨**introspective** [ˌɪntrəˈspektɪv] *adj.* 反省的；内省的
⑩**annoyed** [əˈnɔɪd] *adj.* 恼怒的，气恼的
⑪**drastic** [ˈdræstɪk] *adj.* 极端的；严厉的；急剧的
⑫**modify** [ˈmɒdɪfaɪ] *v.* 修改；减轻；减缓；调节

难句解析

1. Just as a physical mirror serves as the vehicle to reflection, so do all of the people in our lives.

[译文] 就像真正的镜子具有反射功能一样，我们生活中的所有人也都能映射出他人的影子。

[解析] "just as"中的"as"译为"正如"；"serves as"译为"充当"，此处的"as"是"作为"的意思；"so do all of the people in our lives"的结构为"so +助动词+主语"，是部分倒装结构，译为"……也如此"。

2. It means that just as I can get annoyed or disturbed when I notice that aspect in someone else, I better reexamine my qualities and consider making some changes.

[译文] 这意味着，就像我会对其他人身上令我厌恶的特质感到恼怒或不安一样，我应该更好地重新审视自己的特质，并考虑做一些改变。

[解析] "It means that..."整句结构是宾语从句，表达的意思为看到其他人身上的不好的地方，要多反省自己，认识自我，改进自我。

参考译文

镜子，镜子，告诉我

充满爱意的人生活在充满爱意的世界里，充满敌意的人则生活在充满敌意的世界里。你所遇到的每一个人都是你的镜子。

镜子有一个非常独特的功能，那就是映射出在其前面的影像。就像真正的镜子具有反射功能一样，我们生活中的所有人也都能映射出他人的影子。

当我们看到美丽的事物时，例如一座花园，那么这花园就起到了反射作用。为了发现我们面前美好的事物，我们必须能发现自己内在的美。我们爱

某个人，也正是我们爱自己的表现。我们经常听到这样的话："当我和那个人在一起的时候，我爱那时的自己。"这句话也可以简单地说成："在我爱那个人的同时，我也能爱我自己。"有时，我们遇见一个陌生人，感觉仿佛是一见如故，就好像我们已经相识甚久。这种熟悉感可能来自彼此身上的共同点。

就像"镜子"或他人能映射出我们积极的一面一样，我们更有可能注意到映射出自己消极方面的"镜子"。例如，我们很容易就能记住我们碰到自己不太喜欢的人的时刻。我们可能在心里对那个人有些反感。当我们认识不喜欢与之相处的人时，这种情况就更为明显。

具有讽刺意味的是，通常当我们讨厌别人身上的某些特质时，那就说明我们其实讨厌自己身上相类似的特质。

每次，当我遇到不太喜欢的人时，我就开始进一步质问自己。我会扪心自问："我不喜欢那个人的哪些方面？"然后还会问："我是不是有和他相似的地方？"每次，我都能在自己身上看到一些令我厌恶的特质。我有时不得不深刻地反省自己。那么这意味着什么呢？

这意味着，就像我会对其他人身上令我厌恶的特质感到恼怒或不安一样，我应该更好地重新审视自己的特质，并考虑做一些改变。即使我不想做大的改变，至少我会考虑该如何修正自己正在做的一些事情。

我们时常会遇到陌生人，并感到疏远或厌恶。尽管我们不想去相信，不容易也不想去深究，但是弄清楚别人的哪些特质在自己身上有所体现是非常有意义的一课，这也正是增强自我意识的另一个途径。

读后写作

The sentence "just as I can get annoyed or disturbed when I notice that aspect in someone else, I better reexamine my qualities and consider making some changes." has the similar meaning with some ideas in Chinese famous sayings. Please share one of them and express your own opinion about it.

On Immortality in Youth
论青春之不朽

——William Hazlitt

读前导语

　　本篇文章作者威廉·黑兹利特（1778—1830），英国随笔作家。他清晰、直接、男子气概的风格极大地影响了一批随笔作家。他在《莎剧人物》（1817年）、《论英国喜剧作家》（1819年）和《论伊丽莎白时代戏剧文学》（1820年）中的评论研究因可读性和洞察力敏锐而分外知名。这些评论都是收集整理的讲稿。《席间闲谈》，又名《关于人物及风格的新评论》包括了他最典型的部分作品。

　　他在文中写道："年轻时有种永恒的感觉，使我们可以补偿一切。拥有青春的人就好像一尊不朽的神灵。生命的一半时间已经飞逝，另一半还为我们留着，蕴藏着无尽的宝藏；没有划定的界线，我们看到的是无尽的希望和幻想。我们把未来的时代变成我们自己的。"

美文欣赏

　　No young man believes he shall ever die. It was a saying of my brother's, and a fine one. There is a feeling of eternity① in youth, which makes us amend② for everything. To be young is to be as one of the Immortal Gods. One half of time indeed is flown—the other half remains in store for us with all its countless treasures; for there is no line drawn, and we see no limit to our hopes and wishes. We make the coming age our own.

　　The vast, the unbounded③ prospect④ lies before us.

　　Death, old age, are words without a meaning, that pass by us like the idle air which we regard not. Others may have undergone, or may still be liable⑤ to them—we "bear a charmed life", which laughs to scorn⑥ all such sickly fancies. As in setting out on a delightful journey, we strain⑦ our eager gaze forward—bidding the lovely scenes at distance hail—and see no end to the landscape, new objects presenting themselves as we advance; so, in the commencement⑧ of life, we set no bounds to our inclinations⑨, nor to the unrestricted⑩ opportunities of gratifying them. We have as yet found no obstacle, no disposition⑪ to flag; and it seems that we can go on so forever. We look round in a new world, full of life, and motion, at ceaseless⑫ progress; and feel in ourselves all the vigour and spirit to keep pace with it, and do not foresee from any present symptoms how we shall be left behind in the natural course of things, decline into old age, and drop into the grave. It is the simplicity, and as it were abstractedness of our feelings in youth, that (so to seek) identifies us with nature, and (our experience being slight and our passions strong) deludes⑬ us into a belief of being immortal like it. Our short-lives with existence we fondly flatter ourselves, is an indissoluble⑭ and lasting union—a honeymoon that knows neither coldness, jar, nor separation. As infants⑮ smile and sleep, we are rocked in the cradle of our wayward fancies, and lulled⑯ into security by the roar of the universe around us—we quaff the cup of life with eager haste without draining⑰ it, instead of which it only overflows—the more objects press around us, filling the mind with their magnitude⑱ and with the throng of desires that wait upon them, so that we have no room for the thoughts of death.

词汇释义

①**eternity** [ɪˈtɜːnəti] *n.* 永恒；永生，不朽；极长的一段时间

②**amend** [əˈmend] *v.* 修正，修订

③**unbounded** [ʌnˈbaʊndɪd] *adj.* 无限的；无边际的；无节制的

④**prospect** [ˈprɒspekt] *n.* 前景；朝望；眺望处；景象

⑤**liable** [ˈlaɪəbl] *adj.* 有责任的；有义务的；有……倾向的；易……的

⑥**scorn** [skɔːn] *v.* 轻视；看不起；蔑视；嘲笑

⑦**strain** [streɪn] *v.* 拉伤，损伤；尽力；使紧张；拉紧；过滤

⑧**commencement** [kəˈmensmənt] *n.* 开始；毕业典礼

⑨**inclination** [ˌɪnklɪˈneɪʃn] *n.* 倾向；爱好；斜坡

⑩**unrestricted** [ˌʌnrɪˈstrɪktɪd] *adj.* 不受限制的；无限制的

⑪**disposition** [ˌdɪspə'zɪʃn] *n.* 性格；倾向；（财产）赠予，分配

⑫**ceaseless** ['siːsləs] *adj.* 不停的，（好像）无休止的，不断的

⑬**delude** [dɪ'luːd] *v.* 欺骗，哄骗

⑭**indissoluble** [ˌɪndɪ'sɒljəbl] *adj.* 不能分解的

⑮**infant** ['ɪnfənt] *n.* 婴儿，幼儿；未成年人；初学者，生手

⑯**lull** [lʌl] *v.* 使安静，使昏昏欲睡

⑰**drain** [dreɪn] *v.* （使）流干，喝干；使耗尽

⑱**magnitude** ['mægnɪtjuːd] *n.* 巨大，广大；重大，重要；量级

难句解析

1. There is a feeling of eternity in youth, which makes us amend for everything.

【译文】年轻时有种永恒的感觉，使我们可以补偿一切。

【解析】此处"which"引导非限定性定语从句，"amend"译为"补偿，修复"。

2. As in setting out on a delightful journey, we strain our eager gaze forward—bidding the lovely scenes at distance hail—and see no end to the landscape, new objects presenting themselves as we advance; so, in the commencement of life, we set no bounds to our inclinations, nor to the unrestricted opportunities of gratifying them.

【译文】就像踏上愉快的旅程，我们兴奋地极目眺望——向远方的美景欢呼——好风景应接不暇，越往前走，新鲜景致越是美不胜收。同样，年轻的时候，我们听任志趣驰骋，放手让其得到满足。

【解析】"set no bounds to"译为"放纵，听任"。

参考译文

论青春之不朽

没有年轻人认为自己会死亡。这是我兄弟的话，说得不错。年轻时有种永恒的感觉，使我们可以补偿一切。拥有青春的人就好像一尊不朽的神灵。生命的一半时间已经飞逝，另一半还为我们留着，蕴藏着无尽的宝藏；没有划定的界线，我们看到的是无尽的希望和幻想。我们把未来的时代变成我们自己的。

无限辽阔的远景展现在我们面前。

　　死亡、衰老都不过是空话，如同从我们身边吹过的一股风，我们毫不在意。别人可能已经衰老、死亡，或者可能会衰老、死亡——我们"享有着魔法保护的生命"，放声大笑，嘲笑这些脆弱的念头。就像踏上愉快的旅程，我们兴奋地极目眺望——向远方的美景欢呼——好风景应接不暇，越往前走，新鲜景致越是美不胜收。同样，年轻的时候，我们听任志趣驰骋，放手让其得到满足。我们至今还没有遇到过障碍，不知疲倦，意气风发，好像我们会永远如此。我们看到四周一派新天地，生机盎然，变动不息，日新月异，觉得自己充满活力，精神焕发，堪与宇宙并驾齐驱。年轻时没有任何征兆会使我们预见到我们会在事物的自然进程中被甩在后面，迈入老年，进入坟墓。年轻人天性纯真，可以说是茫然无知，总感到青春常在，因而（试图）将自己与大自然画上等号，并且（由于经验缺乏，感情旺盛）总以为自己也能像大自然一样永生。在这个世界上，我们只是暂时栖身，却痴心妄想地把它当作永恒的结合，好像没有冷漠、争吵、离别的蜜月。正像婴儿带着微笑入睡一样，我们躺在用自己一厢情愿的天真幻想所编织的摇篮里，让宇宙的万籁之音把我们催眠；我们兴奋而急切地畅饮生命之杯，怎么也饮不干，似乎永远是满满欲溢的——我们四周万象纷至，灯红酒绿，欲望无穷，我们根本不可能想到死亡。

读后写作

　　How to keep our youth immortal in such a special period? Please give your suggestions.

On Motes and Beams
微尘与栋梁
——William Somerset Maugham

读前导语

本篇文章作者是威廉·萨默塞特·毛姆（1874—1965），英国小说家、剧作家。代表作有戏剧《圈子》，长篇小说《人生的枷锁》《月亮和六便士》，短篇小说集《叶的震颤》《阿金》等。

他在文中写道："让人奇怪的是，和别人的过错比起来，我们自身的过错往往不是那样可恶。我想，其原因应该是我们知晓一切导致自己犯错的情况，因此能够设法谅解自己的错误，而别人的错误却不能谅解。我们对自己的缺点不甚关注，即便是深陷困境而不得不正视它们的时候，我们也会很容易就宽恕自己。据我所知，我们这样做是正确的。缺点是我们自身的一部分，我们必须接纳自己的好和坏。"

美文欣赏

It is curious that our own offenses[①] should seem so much less heinous[②] than the offenses of others. I suppose the reason is that we know all the circumstances that have occasioned[③] them and so manage to excuse in ourselves what we cannot excuse in others. We turn our attention away from our own defects, and when we are forced by untoward events to consider them, find it easy to condone[④] them. For all I know we are right to do this; they are part of us and we must accept the good and bad in ourselves together.

But when we come to judge others, it is not by ourselves as we really are that we

— 62 —

judge them, but by an image that we have formed of ourselves from⑤ which we have left out everything that offends our vanity⑥ or would discredit⑦ us in the eyes of the world. To take a trivial instance: how scornful⑧ we are when we catch someone out telling a lie; but who can say that he has never told not one, but a hundred?

  There is not much to choose between men. They are all a hotchpotch⑨ of greatness and littleness, of virtue and vice, of nobility⑩ and baseness⑪. Some have more strength of character, or more opportunity, and so in one direction or another give their instincts⑫ freer play, but potentially⑬ they are the same. For my part, I do not think I am any better or any worse than most people, but I know that if I set down every action in my life and every thought that has crossed my mind, the world would consider me a monster of depravity⑭. The knowledge that these reveries⑮ are common to all men should inspire one with tolerance to oneself as well as to others. It is well also if they enable us to look upon our fellows, even the most eminent⑯ and respectable, with humor, and if they lead us to take ourselves not too seriously.

词汇释义

①**offense** [əˈfens] *n.* 进攻；攻势；冒犯

②**heinous** [ˈheɪnəs] *adj.* （道德或行为）极邪恶的，极可耻的

③**occasion** [əˈkeɪʒn] *v.* 导致；引起

④**condone** [kənˈdəʊn] *vt.* 容忍，宽恕，原谅

⑤**fro** [frəʊ] *adv.* 来回地，往复地

⑥**vanity** [ˈvænəti] *n.* 虚荣，浮华；自负；空虚，无聊的事物

⑦**discredit** [dɪsˈkredɪt] *v.* 使不可置信；拒绝相信

⑧**scornful** [ˈskɔːnfl] *adj.* 鄙视的，轻蔑的；傲慢的

⑨**hotchpotch** [ˈhɒtʃpɒtʃ] *n.* 杂烩；全家福；大杂烩

⑩**nobility** [nəʊˈbɪləti] *n.* 贵族；高尚的品质；高贵，崇高

⑪**baseness** [ˈbeɪsnəs] *n.* 卑鄙，下贱

⑫**instinct** [ˈɪnstɪŋkt] *n.* 本能，天性；冲动；天资，天才

⑬**potentially** [pəˈtenʃəli] *adv.* 潜在地；可能地

⑭**depravity** [dɪˈprævəti] *n.* 堕落；腐败；恶行；堕落腐化的行为

⑮**reverie** [ˈrevəri] *n.* 想入非非；白日梦；冥想

⑯**eminent** [ˈemɪnənt] *adj.* 卓越的；杰出的；著名的

难句解析

1. It is curious that our own offenses should seem so much less heinous than the offenses of others.

[译文] 让人奇怪的是，和别人的过错比起来，我们自身的过错往往不是那样可恶。

[解析] "It is curious that …"译为"让人奇怪的是，……"。"offense"译为"过错，失误"。

2. The knowledge that these reveries are common to all men should inspire one with tolerance to oneself as well as to others.

[译文] 每个人都会有这样的怪念头，这样的认识应当能够启发我们宽容自己，也宽容他人。

[解析] "knowledge"此处译为"念头，想法"；"as well as"译为"也，和"。

参考译文

微尘与栋梁

让人奇怪的是，和别人的过错比起来，我们自身的过错往往不是那样可恶。我想，其原因应该是我们知晓一切导致自己犯错的情况，因此能够设法谅解自己的错误，而别人的错误却不能谅解。我们对自己的缺点不甚关注，即便是深陷困境而不得不正视它们的时候，我们也会很容易就宽恕自己。据我所知，我们这样做是正确的。缺点是我们自身的一部分，我们必须接纳自己的好和坏。

但是当我们评判别人的时候，情况就不同了。我们不是通过真实的自我来评判别人，而是用一种自我形象来评判，这种自我形象完全摒弃了在任何世人眼中会伤害到自己的虚荣或者体面的东西。举一个小例子来说：当觉察到别人说谎时，我们是多么地蔑视他啊！但是，谁能够说自己从未说过谎？可能还不止一百次呢。

人和人之间没什么大的差别。他们皆是伟大与渺小、善良与邪恶、高尚与低俗的混合体。有的人性格比较坚毅，机会也比较多，因而在这个或那个方面，能够更自由地发挥自己的禀赋，但是人类的潜能却都是相同的。至于我自己，我认为自己并不比大多数人更好或者更差，但是我知道，假如我记下我生命中每一次举动和每一个掠过我脑海的想法的话，世界就会将我视为一个邪恶的怪物。每个人都会有这样的怪念头，这样的认识应当能够启发我们宽容自己，也宽容他人。同时，假如因此我们得以用幽默的态度看待他人，即使是天下最优秀、最令人尊敬的人，而且假如我们也因此不把自己看得过于重要，那是很有裨益的。

读后写作

Every individual matters. Every individual has a role to play. Every individual makes a difference. No matter who you are, you need to do something for society. Please share a tiny thing you did that has a big/special influence on others.

15 Man and Nature
人与自然
——Hamilton Wright Mabie

读前导语

本篇文章作者汉密尔顿·赖特·梅比（1846—1916），美国散文家、编辑、评论家和讲师。

他在文中写道："天空照耀着所有的人，但只有少数人能看到其气象万千的壮丽，他们在每一个午夜的天空都能看出一种蕴含着创造性能量的庄严肃穆之美，无论那种景象重复多少次，都不会使美黯淡失色。"

美文欣赏

The intimacy[①] between man and Nature began with the birth of man on the earth, and becomes each century more intelligent and far-reaching[②]. To Nature, therefore, we turn as to the oldest and most influential[③] teacher of our race; from one point of view once our task-master, now our servant; from another point of view, our constant friend, instructor and inspirer[④].

The very intimacy of this relation robs it of a certain mystery[⑤] and richness, which it would have for all minds if it were the reward of the few instead of being the privilege[⑥] of the many.

To the few it is, in every age, full of wonder and beauty; to the many it is a matter of course. The heavens shine for all, but they have a changing splendor[⑦] to those only who see in every midnight sky a majesty of creative energy and resource, which no repetition of the spectacle[⑧] can dim.

If the stars shone but once in a thousand years, men would gaze, awe-struck and worshipful⑨, on a vision which is not less but more wonderful because it shines nightly above the whole earth.

In like manner, and for the same reason, we become indifferent⑩ to that delicately⑪ beautiful or sublimely⑫ impressive sky scenery, which the clouds form and reform, compose and dissipate⑬, a thousand times on a summer day. The mystery, the terror, and the music of the sea; the secret and subduing⑭ charm of the woods, so full of healing for the spent mind or the restless spirit; the majesty of the hills, holding in their recesses the secrets of light and atmosphere; the infinite⑮ variety of landscape, never imitative or repetitious⑯, but always appealing to the imagination with some fresh and unsuspected⑰ loveliness—who feels the full power of these marvelous⑱ resources for the enrichment of life, or takes from them all the health, delight, and enrichment they have to bestow⑲?

词汇释义

①**intimacy** [ˈɪntɪməsi] *n.* 亲密；亲近；亲昵的言行

②**far-reaching** [ˌfɑːˈriːtʃɪŋ] *adj.* 深远的，广泛的，深至远处的

③**influential** [ˌɪnfluˈenʃl] *adj.* 有影响力的；有支配力的

④**inspirer** [ɪnˈspaɪərə(r)] *n.* 启发灵感、鼓舞（或激励）人心的人

⑤**mystery** [ˈmɪstri] *n.* 秘密，谜；神秘，神秘的事物

⑥**privilege** [ˈprɪvəlɪdʒ] *n.* 特权；优惠；荣幸

⑦**splendor** [ˈsplendə(r)] *n.* 华丽；壮丽；光辉；显赫

⑧**spectacle** [ˈspektəkl] *n.* 奇观，壮观；光景，景象

⑨**worshipful** [ˈwɜːʃɪpfl] *adj.* 可敬的，尊敬的

⑩**indifferent** [ɪnˈdɪfrənt] *adj.* 漠不关心的；一般的

⑪**delicately** [ˈdelɪkətli] *adv.* 优美地，精致地，微妙地

⑫**sublimely** [səˈblaɪmli] *adv.* 高尚地，卓越地

⑬**dissipate** [ˈdɪsɪpeɪt] *v.* 驱散；消散；浪费，挥霍；耗尽

⑭**subdue** [səbˈdjuː] *v.* 征服；克制；制服

⑮**infinite** [ˈɪnfɪnət] *adj.* 无限的，无穷的；极大的，极多的

⑯**repetitious** [ˌrepəˈtɪʃəs] *adj.* 重复的，反复的

⑰**unsuspected** [ˌʌnsəˈspektɪd] *adj.* 未被怀疑的，无嫌疑的
⑱**marvelous** [ˈmɑːvələs] *adj.* 引起惊异的；不可思议的
⑲**bestow** [bɪˈstəʊ] *vt.* 赠给，授予；放置，安置，贮藏

难句解析

1. To Nature, therefore, we turn as to the oldest and most influential teacher of our race; from one point of view once our task-master, now our servant; from another point of view, our constant friend, instructor and inspirer.

译文 因此，我们把自然当作我们人类最年长、最有影响力的老师看待；从一种观点看，自然曾经是我们的监工，现在成了我们的奴仆；从另一种观点看，自然是我们永恒的朋友、导师和启发者。

解析 "therefore" 此处为插入语，表示"因此"之意；"from one point of view…, from another point of view…" 是说明两种观点时常用的结构。

2. In like manner, and for the same reason, we become indifferent to that delicately beautiful or sublimely impressive sky scenery, which the clouds form and reform, compose and dissipate, a thousand times on a summer day.

译文 夏日的天空，浮云千百次地聚散飘忽，变幻着柔美壮丽的动人画卷，而我们，同样地，也因为相同的原因，都无动于衷，熟视无睹。

解析 "become indifferent to" 表示"对……漠不关心，冷漠"，"delicately beautiful" 和 "sublimely impressive" 两个短语描绘出了天空之美，与我们的态度形成对比。

参考译文

人与自然

自人类在地球上出现，人与自然的亲密关系也就随之诞生了，而且这种关系一个世纪比一个世纪更加睿智，影响更加深远。因此，我们把自然当作我们人类最年长、最有影响力的老师看待；从一种观点看，自然曾经是我们的监工，现在成了我们的奴仆；从另一种观点看，自然是我们永恒的朋友、导师和启发者。

这种亲密关系，如果仅仅是少数人的奖赏，而不是大多数人享有的权

利,那对于众人来说,就会失去神秘的丰饶。

在每个时代,对于少数人,自然充满了奇妙和美好的东西;对于多数人,自然只是普通的存在,平平常常。天空照耀着所有的人,但只有少数人能看到其气象万千的壮丽,他们在每一个午夜的天空都能看出一种蕴含着创造性能量的庄严肃穆之美,无论那种景象重复多少次,都不会使美黯淡失色。

如果星辰每一千年才照耀一次大地,人们将怀着敬畏崇敬的心情凝视那种美景,而美景夜夜出现在人间大地,其实非但不会有所减损,反而会更添奇妙。

夏日的天空,浮云千百次地聚散飘忽,变幻着柔美壮丽的动人画卷,而我们,同样地,也因为相同的原因,都无动于衷,熟视无睹。神秘、恐怖而富有乐感的海洋;森林摄人魂魄的魅力与神秘,蕴含抚慰疲惫与焦躁之心的灵丹妙药;肃穆静美的山峦,在其幽深之处,饱含光与大气之奥秘;变幻无穷的风景,永远以出人意料的新鲜美丽唤起人们的想象力——谁感受到了这些奇妙资源的全部力量,让生活更加充盈富足?或者,谁从那里领受了自然所赐予的所有健康、快乐和丰美?

读后写作

Nature is an excellent teacher for our human beings. Actually, sometimes, we don't protect it very well. Please write a passage to share your opinion on environmental protection.

Three Passions in My Life
我生命中的三种激情
——Bertrand Russell

读前导语

本篇文章作者伯特兰·罗素（1872—1970），英国哲学家、数学家、逻辑学家、历史学家、文学家，分析哲学的主要创始人，世界和平运动的倡导者和组织者，主要作品有《西方哲学史》《哲学问题》《心的分析》《物的分析》等。

他在文中写道："爱的力量和知识的力量引我接近天堂，但同情之心往往又把我拉回大地。痛苦的哭泣回响、震荡在我的心中。饥饿的儿童，被压迫、受折磨的人们，成为儿孙们讨厌的包袱的、无助的老人们，充斥着整个世界的孤独的气氛、贫穷和苦难，所有这一切都是对人类生活原本该具有的样子的讽刺。我渴望消除一切邪恶，但我办不到，因为我自己也处于苦难之中。"

美文欣赏

Three passions, simple but overwhelmingly① strong, have governed my life: the longing for love, the search for knowledge, and unbearable pity for the suffering of mankind. These passions, like great winds, have blown me hither② and thither, in a wayward course, over a deep ocean of anguish③, reaching to the very verge④ of despair.

I have sought love, first, because it brings ecstasy⑤—ecstasy so great that I would often have sacrificed all the rest of life for a few hours of this joy. I have sought it, next, because it relieves loneliness—that terrible loneliness in which one shivering⑥ consciousness looks over the rim of the world into the cold unfathomable⑦ lifeless abyss. I have sought it, finally, because in the union of love I have seen, in a mystic miniature⑧, the prefiguring⑨ vision of the heaven that saints and poets have imagined. This is what I sought, and though it might seem too good for human life, this is what at last I have found.

With equal passion I have sought knowledge. I have wished to understand the hearts of men. I have wished to know why the stars shine. I have tried to apprehend⑩ the Pythagorean power by which number holds sway above the flux. A little of this, but not much, I have achieved.

Love and knowledge, so far as they were possible, led upward toward the heavens. But always pity brought me back to earth. Echoes of cries of pain reverberate⑪ in my heart. Children in famine, victims⑫ tortured by oppressors⑬, helpless old people a hated burden to their sons, and the whole world of loneliness, poverty, and pain make a mockery⑭ of what human life should be. I long to alleviate⑮ the evil, but I cannot, and I too suffer.

This has been my life. I have found it worth living, and would gladly live it again if the chance were offered me.

词汇释义

①**overwhelmingly** [ˌəʊvə(r)'welmɪŋli] adv. 压倒地，无法抵抗地

②**hither** ['hɪðə(r)] adv. 到此处，向此处

③**anguish** ['æŋgwɪʃ] n. 剧痛，悲痛；苦恼

④**verge** [vɜːdʒ] n. 边，边缘；界限；范围；绿地

⑤**ecstasy** ['ekstəsi] n. 狂喜；出神，忘形；无法自控的情绪

⑥**shivering** ['ʃɪvərɪŋ] adj. 颤抖的

⑦**unfathomable** [ʌn'fæðəməbl] adj. 高深莫测的，难以了解的

⑧**miniature** ['mɪnɪtʃə(r)] n. 微型复制品；微小模型；微型画

⑨**prefigure** [ˌpriː'fɪɡə(r)] vt. 预示，预想

⑩**apprehend** [ˌæprɪ'hend] v. 理解；逮捕，拘押；忧虑

⑪**reverberate** [rɪ'vɜːbəreɪt] v. 回响；弹回；反射

⑫**victim** ['vɪktɪm] n. 受害者，遇难者；祭品，牺牲品

⑬**oppressor** [ə'presə(r)] n. 压迫者，暴君

⑭**mockery** ['mɒkəri] n. 嘲笑，愚弄；笑柄；（拙劣的）模仿

⑮**alleviate** [ə'liːvieɪt] v. 减轻；缓解

难句解析

1. Three passions, simple but overwhelmingly strong, have governed my life: the longing for love, the search for knowledge, and unbearable pity for the suffering of mankind.

译文 三种激情虽然简单，却异常强烈，它们统治着我的生命，那便是：对爱的渴望、对知识的追求，以及对人类苦难的难以承受的同情。

解析 "simple but overwhelmingly strong" 充当插入语，对 "three passions" 进行修饰和限定，"govern" 一词写出了 "three passions" 对于我生命的意义重大。

2. Echoes of cries of pain reverberate in my heart. Children in famine, victims tortured by oppressors, helpless old people a hated burden to their sons, and the whole world of loneliness, poverty, and pain make a mockery of what human life should be.

译文 痛苦的哭泣回响、震荡在我的心中。饥饿的儿童，被压迫、受折磨的人们，成为儿孙们讨厌的包袱的、无助的老人们，充斥着整个世界的孤独的气氛、贫穷和苦难，所有这一切都是对人类生活原本该具有的样子的讽刺。

解析 本句生动形象地描绘出我对这些 poor people 的同情，同情他们，为他们做一些我能做的事情是我生命中的热情之一，也是我生命的意义。

参考译文

我生命中的三种激情

三种激情虽然简单，却异常强烈，它们统治着我的生命，那便是：对爱的渴望、对知识的追求，以及对人类苦难的难以承受的同情。这三种激情像变化莫测的狂风任意地把我刮来刮去，把我刮入痛苦的深海，到了绝望的边缘。

我曾经寻找爱，首先是因为它能使我欣喜若狂——这种喜悦之情如此强烈，使我常常宁愿为这几个小时的愉悦而牺牲生命中的其他一切。我寻求爱，其次是因为爱能解除孤独——在这种可怕的孤独中，一颗颤抖的良心在世界的边缘，注视着下面冰凉、毫无生气、望不见底的深渊。我寻求爱，还因为在爱的融合中，我能以某种神秘的图像看到曾被圣人和诗人想象过的天堂里未来的景象。这就是我所追求的东西，虽然这似乎对于人类的生命来说过于完美，但这确实是我最终发现的东西。

我怀着同样的激情去寻找知识，我曾渴望着理解人心，我曾渴望知道为何星星会闪烁，我还企图弄懂毕达哥拉斯所谓的用数字控制变化的力量，但在这方面，我只知道一点点。

爱的力量和知识的力量引我接近天堂，但同情之心往往又把我拉回大地。痛苦的哭泣回响、震荡在我的心中。饥饿的儿童，被压迫、受折磨的人们，成为儿孙们讨厌的包袱的、无助的老人们，充斥着整个世界的孤独的气氛、贫穷和苦难，所有这一切都是对人类生活原本该具有的样子的讽刺。我渴望消除一切邪恶，但我办不到，因为我自己也处于苦难之中。

这就是我的生活，我认为值得一过。而且，如果有第二次机会，我将乐意地再过一次。

读后写作

Life is only once for everyone and it is limited. What is the passion in your life?

The Delights of Reading
读书之乐
——Sir John Lubbock

读前导语

本篇文章作者约翰·卢伯克（1834—1913）生于英国伦敦，是享有盛誉的考古学家、生物学家和政治家。1865 年，他首先提出旧石器时代和新石器时代这两个名词。他一生留有 3 部著作：《史前时代》《蚂蚁、蜜蜂和黄蜂》《人生的乐趣》。其中《人生的乐趣》是他的一部休闲之作，在国外再版 20 次，意外地成就了这位著名科学家在文学领域的卓越名声。

他在文中写道："书籍之于人类，犹如记忆之于个人。书籍既可记录人种之演变，亦可记载人类之发现；既有日积月累之知识，亦不乏世代相传之经验；书籍之于人类，可描绘自然之奇迹与美丽，于困难无助之际予以提携，于悲伤痛苦之时施以抚慰；让困倦之时刻变为欢乐之时光，让头脑充满丰富之想象，让心灵布满美好快乐之思想，恃此而人可走出自我，超越自我。"

美文欣赏

Books are to mankind what memory is to the individual①. They contain the history of our race, the discoveries we have made, the accumulated② knowledge and experience of ages; they picture for us the marvels③ and beauties of nature, help us in our difficulties, comfort us in sorrow and in suffering, change hours of weariness④ into moments of delight, store our minds with ideas, fill them with good and happy thoughts, and lift us out of and above ourselves.

There is an oriental⑤ story of two men: one was a king, who every night dreamed he was a beggar; the other was a beggar, who every night dreamed he was a prince and lived in a palace. I am not sure that the king had very much the best of it. Imagination is sometimes more vivid than reality. But, however this may be, when we read we may not only (if we wish it) be kings and live in palaces, but, what is far better, we may transport ourselves to the mountains or the seashore, and visit the most beautiful parts of the earth, without fatigue[6], inconvenience, or expense[7].

Macaulay[8] had wealth and fame, rank and power, and yet he tells us in his biography[9] that he owed the happiest hours of his life to books. In a charming letter to a little girl, he says, "Thank you for your very pretty letter. I am always glad to make my little girl happy, and nothing pleases me so much as to see that she likes books, for when she is as old as I am, she will find that they are better than all the tarts and cakes, toys and plays, and sights in the world. If any one would make me the greatest king that ever lived, with palaces and gardens and fine dinners, and wines and coaches, and beautiful clothes, and hundreds of servants, on condition that I should not read books, I would not be a king. I would rather be a poor man in a garret with plenty of books than a king who did not love reading."

Precious and priceless are the blessings which the books scatter[10] around our daily paths. We walk, in imagination, with the noblest spirits, through the most sublime[11] and enchanting[12] regions.

词汇释义

①**individual** [ˌɪndɪˈvɪdʒuəl] *adj.* 单独的；个人的；独特的 *n.* 个人，个体

②**accumulate** [əˈkjuːmjəleɪt] *v.* 积累，积聚；堆积

③**marvel** [ˈmɑːvl] *n.* 奇迹；令人惊奇的事物（或事例）

④**weariness** [ˈwɪərinəs] *n.* 疲倦；厌倦

⑤**oriental** [ˌɔːriˈentl] *adj.* 东方的；东方人的；东方文化的

⑥**fatigue** [fəˈtiːɡ] *n.* 疲劳，厌倦；（士兵）工作服

⑦**expense** [ɪkˈspens] *n.* 开销；费用；业务费

⑧**Macaulay** [məˈkɔːli] 麦考利（姓氏）

⑨**biography** [baɪˈɒɡrəfi] *n.* 传记；传记作品

⑩**scatter** [ˈskætə(r)] *v.* 播撒；散开；（使）分散

⑪**sublime** ［səˈblaɪm］ *adj.* 庄严的；雄伟的；令人赞叹的；极端的

⑫**enchanting** ［ɪnˈtʃɑːntɪŋ］ *adj.* 使人喜悦的；妩媚的；迷人的

难句解析

1. But, however this may be, when we read we may not only (if we wish it) be kings and live in palaces, but, what is far better, we may transport ourselves to the mountains or the seashore, and visit the most beautiful parts of the earth, without fatigue, inconvenience, or expense.

译文 是否如此，姑且不论，然读书时，恁可想象自己即为国王，居宫殿；且读书乃美差之事：既可使人纵情山川，嬉戏海滩，亦可使人遍访世之美景；既可使人除身心疲惫之虑，亦可使人解囊中羞涩之忧。

解析 "transport... to..."译为"把……转换成……"；"we may transport ourselves to the mountains or the seashore, and visit the most beautiful parts of the earth, without fatigue, inconvenience, or expense"写出了我在读书过程中获得的快乐和收获。

2. If any one would make me the greatest king that ever lived, with palaces and gardens and fine dinners, and wines and coaches, and beautiful clothes, and hundreds of servants, on condition that I should not read books, I would not be a king.

译文 若有人请余当史上最伟大之国王，享宫殿花园之乐，品美味佳肴，驾华车着丽服，差数以百计之奴仆，唯无读书之条件，余宁可弃做国王，而做穷人，居斗室，享书无数，亦勿做厌书之国王。

解析 "If any one would ..." "on condition that...（译为"只要……"）" "I would not be..." 使用了虚拟语气表达我对读书的执念。

参考译文

读书之乐

书籍之于人类，犹如记忆之于个人。书籍既可记录人种之演变，亦可记载人类之发现；既有日积月累之知识，亦不乏世代相传之经验；书籍之于人类，可描绘自然之奇迹与美丽，于困难无助之际予以提携，于悲伤痛苦之时施以抚慰；让困倦之时刻变为欢乐之时光，让头脑充满丰富之想象，让心灵布满美好快乐之思想，恃此而人可走出自我，超越自我。

有一东方典故，言及二人：一为国王，一为乞丐。国王夜必有恶魇，魇中成乞丐；乞丐晚必做美梦，梦中变王子，居宫殿。国王是否泰然处之，余不敢肯定。想象之于现实或更栩栩然。是否如此，姑且不论，然读书时，恣可想象自己即为国王，居宫殿；且读书乃美差之事：既可使人纵情山川，嬉戏海滩，亦可使人遍访世之美景；既可使人除身心疲惫之虑，亦可使人解囊中羞涩之忧。

麦考利既有财富与名望，亦有地位与权力，然其传记曰，其一生最快乐之时光在于读书。麦考利尝书信一封于一女童，曰："来信收悉，内容精彩，深表感谢。悉知汝喜好读书，且能乐焉。余倍感欣慰，若到吾今日之年岁，汝定会晓解，较之于馅饼与蛋糕，较之于玩具与游戏，较之于世之名胜风景，读书之乐远胜焉。若有人请余当史上最伟大之国王，享宫殿花园之乐，品美味佳肴，驾华车着丽服，差数以百计之奴仆，唯无读书之条件，余宁可弃做国王，而做穷人，居斗室，享书无数，亦勿做厌书之国王。"

有书则有福，且其贵无价，无时不在，无处莫有。有书，则可驰骋想象，畅游美景胜地。

读后写作

Reading is valuable to our life. We can enjoy ourselves in reading and get what we want in it. What is your feeling when reading books? Please share it with us.

The Happy Door
快乐之门
——Mildred Cram

读前导语

本篇文章作者米尔德里德·克拉姆（1889—1985）是一位编剧，主要作品有《爱情故事》《爱与死》《金玉盟》《除了明天》等。

她在文中写道："快乐是一种意外的收获，但保持快乐却是一种成就，一种灵性的胜利。努力追寻快乐并不自私，实际上，这是我们对自己和他人应尽的责任。不快乐就像传染病，它使得人们都躲避不快乐的人。不快乐的人很快就会发现自己处于孤独、悲惨、痛苦的境地。然而，有一种简单得看似荒谬的治病良方：如果你不快乐，就假装你很快乐！"

美文欣赏

Happiness is like a pebble① dropped into a pool to set in motion an ever-widening circle of ripples②. As Stevenson has said, being happy is a duty.

There is no exact definition③ of the word happiness. Happy people are happy for all sorts of reasons. The key is not wealth or physical well-being, since we find beggars, invalids④ and so-called failures, who are extremely happy.

Being happy is a sort of unexpected dividend⑤. But staying happy is an accomplishment⑥, a triumph⑦ of soul and character. It is not selfish to strive⑧ for it. It is, indeed, a duty to ourselves and others.

Being unhappy is like an infectious⑨ disease. It causes people to shrink⑩ away from the sufferer. He soon finds himself alone, miserable⑪ and embittered⑫. There is, however, a cure so simple as to seem, at first glance, ridiculous⑬; if you don't feel happy, pretend to be!

It works. Before long you will find that instead of repelling⑭ people, you attract them. You discover how deeply rewarding it is to be the center of wider and wider circles of good will.

Then the make-believe becomes a reality. You possess the secret of peace of mind, and can forget yourself in being of service to others.

Being happy, once it is realized as a duty and established⑮ as a habit, opens doors into unimaginable gardens thronged⑯ with grateful friends.

词汇释义

①**pebble** ['pebl] *n.* 卵石；水晶透镜；卵石花纹

②**ripple** ['rɪpl] *n.* 涟漪，涟波

③**definition** [ˌdefɪ'nɪʃn] *n.* 定义，释义；清晰（度）

④**invalid** [ɪn'vælɪd] *n.* 病人，病号；残废者；伤病军人

⑤**dividend** ['dɪvɪdend] *n.* 红利，股息

⑥**accomplishment** [ə'kʌmplɪʃmənt] *n.* 成就，成绩；完成，实现

⑦**triumph** ['traɪʌmf] *n.* 胜利；巨大的成就；典范

⑧**strive** [straɪv] *v.* 努力奋斗，力求；斗争，力争

⑨**infectious** [ɪn'fekʃəs] *adj.* 传染的；有传染性的；易传染的

⑩**shrink** [ʃrɪŋk] *v.* 收缩；畏缩

⑪**miserable** ['mɪzrəbl] *adj.* 悲惨的；令人痛苦的；太少的；脾气坏的

⑫**embitter** [ɪm'bɪtə(r)] *vt.* 使怨恨，激怒

⑬**ridiculous** [rɪ'dɪkjələs] *adj.* 荒谬的；愚蠢的；可笑的

⑭**repel** [rɪ'pel] *vt.* 击退；使厌恶；抵制；使不愉快；排斥

⑮**establish** [ɪ'stæblɪʃ] *v.* 创建；建立（尤指正式关系）；证实

⑯**throng** [θrɒŋ] *v.* 群集；蜂拥而至；挤满

难句解析

1. The key is not wealth or physical well-being, since we find beggars, invalids and so-called failures, who are extremely happy.

译文 快乐的关键并不是财富或身体健康，因为我们发现有些乞丐、残疾人和所谓的失败者也都非常快乐。

解析 "key"在此处译为"关键"；"invalids"在此处的意思是"残疾人"；本句使用"beggars, invalids and so-called failures"表示一些我们平时认为的社会中不会快乐的人，他们虽然并不富有、身有缺陷，但依然享受着人生的快乐。

2. Being happy is a sort of unexpected dividend. But staying happy is an accomplishment, a triumph of soul and character.

译文 快乐是一种意外的收获，但保持快乐却是一种成就，一种灵性的胜利。

解析 "a sort of unexpected dividend"表示在生活中快乐是令人感到意外的，但保持快乐对于任何人来说都是一种成就和胜利。

参考译文

快乐之门

快乐就像一块为了激起阵阵涟漪而丢进池塘的小石头。正如史蒂文森所说，快乐是一种责任。

快乐这个词并没有确切的定义，快乐的人快乐的理由多种多样。快乐的关键并不是财富或身体健康，因为我们发现有些乞丐、残疾人和所谓的失败者也都非常快乐。

快乐是一种意外的收获，但保持快乐却是一种成就，一种灵性的胜利。努力追寻快乐并不自私，实际上，这是我们对自己和他人应尽的责任。

不快乐就像传染病，它使得人们都躲避不快乐的人。不快乐的人很快就会发现自己处于孤独、悲惨、痛苦的境地。然而，有一种简单得看似荒谬的治病良方：如果你不快乐，就假装你很快乐！

这很有效。不久你就会发现，别人不再躲着你了，相反，你开始吸引别人了。你会发觉，做一块能激起好意涟漪的小石头有多么值得。

然后假装就变成了现实。你拥有了使心灵平静的秘密，会因帮助他人而忘我。

一旦你认识到快乐是一种责任并使快乐成为习惯，通向不可思议的乐园的大门就会向你敞开，那里满是感激你的朋友。

读后写作

As some people say, the older they become, the less happiness they get. Do you agree with it?

The Love of Beauty
爱 美
——John Ruskin

读前导语

本篇文章作者约翰·罗斯金（1819—1900），英国作家、艺术家、艺术评论家，维多利亚时代艺术趣味的代言人。

他在文中写道："美，在春日百花中绽放；美，在绿叶嫩枝间摇曳；美，在深海幽谷里游弋；美，在奇石与贝壳的缤纷色彩中闪烁。不只是这些细微之物，还有海洋、山川、云彩、繁星、日升日落，一切都洋溢着美。"

美文欣赏

The love of beauty is an essential① part of all healthy human nature. It is a moral② quality. The absence of it is not an assured ground of condemnation③, but the presence of it is an invariable sign of goodness of heart. In proportion④ to the degree in which it is felt will probably be the degree in which nobleness and beauty of character will be attained⑤.

Natural beauty is an all-pervading⑥ presence. The universe is its temple. It unfolds into the numberless flowers of spring. It waves in the branches of trees and the green blades of grass. It haunts the depths of the earth and the sea. It gleams⑦ from the hues of the shell and the precious stone. And not only these minute objects but the oceans, the mountains, the clouds, the stars, the rising and the setting sun—all overflow with beauty. This beauty is so precious, and so congenial⑧ to our tenderest and noblest feelings, that it is painful to think of the multitude⑨ of people living in the midst of it and yet remaining almost blind to it.

All persons should seek to become acquainted⑩ with the beauty in nature. There is not a worm we tread upon, nor a leaf that dances merrily as it falls before the autumn winds, but calls for our study and admiration. The power to appreciate beauty not merely increases our sources of happiness—it enlarges our moral nature, too. Beauty calms our restlessness and dispels⑪ our cares. Go into the fields or the woods, spend a summer day by the sea or the mountains, and all your little perplexities⑫ and anxieties will vanish⑬. Listen to sweet music, and your foolish fears and petty jealousies⑭ will pass away. The beauty of the world helps us to seek and find the beauty of goodness.

词汇释义

①**essential** [ɪˈsenʃl] *adj.* 基本的；必不可少的；根本的

②**moral** [ˈmɒrəl] *n.* 道德；寓意 *adj.* 有关道德的；有道德的

③**condemnation** [ˌkɒndemˈneɪʃn] *n.* 谴责，指责

④**proportion** [prəˈpɔːʃn] *n.* 部分，份额；比例；重要性；均衡

⑤**attain** [əˈteɪn] *v.* 获得；达到

⑥**all-pervading** [ˌɔːl pəˈveɪdɪŋ] *adj.* 普及的，普遍的

⑦**gleam** [gliːm] *v.* 闪烁，闪亮

⑧**congenial** [kənˈdʒiːniəl] *adj.* 意气相投的；性格相似的

⑨**multitude** [ˈmʌltɪtjuːd] *n.* 大量，许多；大众，人群

⑩**acquainted** [əˈkweɪntɪd] *adj.* 了解的，熟悉的；认识的

⑪**dispel** [dɪˈspel] *v.* 消除；驱散；驱逐

⑫**perplexity** [pəˈpleksəti] *n.* 困惑；混乱；复杂；困难

⑬**vanish** [ˈvænɪʃ] *v.* 消失，突然不见；灭绝，不存在

⑭**jealousy** [ˈdʒeləsi] *n.* 妒忌，猜忌；戒备，小心提防

> 难句解析

1. In proportion to the degree in which it is felt will probably be the degree in which nobleness and beauty of character will be attained.

[译文] 品德的高尚与美好所达到的程度可能与对美的感受程度成正比。

[解析] "in proportion to"译为"成比例，按比例"；"nobleness and beauty of character"译为"品德的高尚与美好"。

2. There is not a worm we tread upon, nor a leaf that dances merrily as it falls before the autumn winds, but calls for our study and admiration.

[译文] 没有一条我们踩过的小虫，没有一片在秋风拂掠之际飞舞的树叶不值得我们研究与赞赏。

[解析] "There is not ..., nor..."此处理解为"没有……，也没有……"；"call for"本义为"招募，征集"，此处引申为"号召"。

> 参考译文

爱　美

爱美是整个健全人性不可或缺之一部分。它是一种道德品质。缺乏这种品质并不能作为受到责难的充分理由，但是拥有这种品质则是心灵美好的永恒标志。品德的高尚与美好所达到的程度可能与对美的感受程度成正比。

大自然的美无处不在，整个宇宙就是美的殿堂。美，在春日百花中绽放；美，在绿叶嫩枝间摇曳；美，在深海幽谷里游弋；美，在奇石与贝壳的缤纷色彩中闪烁。不只是这些细微之物，还有海洋、山川、云彩、繁星、日升日落，一切都洋溢着美。这样的美是如此珍贵，与我们最温柔、最高尚的情愫是如此相宜。然而，想到很多人置身于美之中，却几乎对它熟视无睹，真是令人痛心不已。

所有的人都应该去认识大自然之美。没有一条我们踩过的小虫，没有一片在秋风拂掠之际飞舞的树叶不值得我们研究与赞赏。欣赏美的能力不仅增加了我们快乐的来源，也加强了我们德性的修养。美使我们不安的心平静下来，也驱散了我们的忧虑。到田野或森林去，在夏日的海边或山上待上一天，那么你所有微不足道的困惑与焦虑都会烟消云散。倾听悦耳的音乐，你那愚蠢的恐惧与狭隘的嫉妒都会过去。世界之美将有助于我们找到为善之美。

读后写作

Everyone has a love for beauty. Being beautiful is a common topic and a pursue for us. So can you share the way you keep beautiful in you mind?

The Man in Old Age
人生之暮年
——Bertrand Russell

读前导语

本篇文章作者伯特兰·罗素（1872—1970），英国哲学家、数学家、逻辑学家、历史学家、文学家，分析哲学的主要创始人，世界和平运动的倡导者和组织者，主要作品有《西方哲学史》《哲学问题》《心的分析》《物的分析》等。

他在书中写道："人生就像一条河，开头河面狭小，夹于两岸之间，河水奔腾咆哮，流过巨石，飞下悬崖。后来，河面渐渐开阔起来，两岸相隔越来越远，河水也流得较为平缓，最后汇入大海，与海水浑然一体，结束了其单独存在的那一段历程，融入自然的大美之中。"

美文欣赏

Some old people are oppressed[①] by the fear of death. In the young there is a justification[②] for this feeling. Young men who have reason to fear that they will be killed in battle may justifiably feel bitter in the thought that they have been cheated of the best things that life has to offer. But in an old man who has known human joys and sorrows, and has achieved whatever work it was in him to do, the fear of death is somewhat abject[③] and ignoble[④]. The best way to overcome it—so at least it seems to me—is to make your interests gradually wider and more impersonal[⑤], until bit by bit the walls of the ego recede[⑥], and your life becomes increasingly merged[⑦] in the universal life. An individual human existence should be like a river—small at first, narrowly contained within its banks, and rushing passionately[⑧] past boulders and over waterfalls. Gradually the river grows wider, the banks recede⑨, the waters flow more quietly, and in the end, without any visible break, they become merged in the sea, and can painlessly lose their individual being. The man who, in old age, can see his life in this way, will not suffer from the fear of death, since the things he cares for will continue. And if, with the decay⑩ of vitality⑪, weariness increases, the thought of rest will be not unwelcome. I should wish to die while still at work, knowing that others will carry on what I can no longer do, and content in the thought that what was possible has been done.

词汇释义

①**oppress** [əˈpres] *vt.* 使烦恼，使意气消沉，使气馁，使无精神

②**justification** [ˌdʒʌstɪfɪˈkeɪʃn] *n.* 辩解；无过失；正当的理由

③**abject** [ˈæbdʒekt] *adj.* 卑鄙的，下贱的；凄惨的；被鄙视的

④**ignoble** [ɪɡˈnəʊbl] *adj.* 卑鄙的；可耻的；出身低微的

⑤**impersonal** [ɪmˈpɜːsənl] *adj.* 没有人情味的；和个人无关的

⑥**recede** [rɪˈsiːd] *v.* 后退；减弱；（价值、品质等）跌落

⑦**merged** [mɜːdʒd] *adj.* 合并的

⑧**passionately** [ˈpæʃənətli] *adv.* 热情地，激昂地

⑨**recede** [rɪˈsiːd] *v.* 后退；减弱；跌落，低落，变坏

⑩**decay** [dɪˈkeɪ] *n.* 腐烂，腐朽；衰败

⑪**vitality** [vaɪˈtæləti] *n.* 活力；生气；生命力；热情

难句解析

1. Young men who have reason to fear that they will be killed in battle may justifiably feel bitter in the thought that they have been cheated of the best things that life has to offer.

[译文] 年轻人有理由害怕在战场上被杀死，一想到被剥夺了生命赋予的最好的东西，感到痛苦，倒也在理。

[解析] 本句中"who"引导定语从句，修饰"young men"，在从句中充当主语；句中第二个"that"引导同位语从句，解释说明之前出现的"thought"一词，第三个"that"引导定语从句，修饰"the best things"，在从句中充当宾语。

2. But in an old man who has known human joys and sorrows, and has achieved whatever work it was in him to do, the fear of death is somewhat abject and ignoble.

译文 但是老年人尝遍了人生的酸甜苦辣，对死亡尚有恐惧，这多少有点低贱，不那么光彩。

解析 本句是对饱尝人生酸甜苦辣的老年人展开描述，说他们还对死亡心存恐惧，让他人看起来多少有点低贱和不光彩。

参考译文

人生之暮年

有些老人对死亡深感恐惧。年轻时有此感受情有可原。年轻人有理由害怕在战场上被杀死，一想到被剥夺了生命赋予的最好的东西，感到痛苦，倒也在理。但是老年人尝遍了人生的酸甜苦辣，对死亡尚有恐惧，这多少有点低贱，不那么光彩。最好的解决办法——至少在我看来是这样——是使你的兴趣越来越广，越来越不受个人感情影响，直到自我的壁垒一点点消失，你的生命渐渐融入宇宙万物中。人生就像一条河，开头河面狭小，夹于两岸之间，河水奔腾咆哮，流过巨石，飞下悬崖。后来，河面渐渐开阔起来，两岸相隔越来越远，河水也流得较为平缓，最后汇入大海，与海水浑然一体，结束了其单独存在的那一段历程，融入自然的大美之中。人到晚年，能这样看待生命，就不会为死亡而恐惧，因为他所关爱的东西将继续留存于世。精力已衰，日见倦怠，安然入眠，回归自然，与天地同在，福莫大焉。我愿意自己尚在工作时离开人世，因为我知道别人会继续我已做不了的事情，想到责任已尽，才华已展，便心满意足了。

读后写作

Becoming old is a trend which is not avoidable. Have you ever imagined what you are going to do when you are old?

The True Nobility
真正的高贵
——Ernest Hemingway

读前导语

本篇文章作者欧内斯特·海明威（1899—1961），出生于美国伊利诺伊州芝加哥市郊区奥克帕克，美国作家、记者，被认为是20世纪最著名的小说家之一。1953年，他以《老人与海》一书获得普利策奖；1954年的《老人与海》又为海明威夺得诺贝尔文学奖。2001年，海明威的《太阳照常升起》与《永别了，武器》两部作品被美国现代图书馆列入"20世纪的100部最佳英文小说"。

他在文中写道："悔恨自己的错误，而且力求不再重蹈覆辙，这才是真正的悔悟。优于别人，并不高贵，真正的高贵应该是优于过去的自己。"

美文欣赏

In a calm sea every man is a pilot.

But all sunshine without shade, all pleasure without pain, is not life at all. Take the lot of the happiest—it is a tangled① yarn②. Bereavements③ and blessings, one following another, make us sad and blessed by turns. Even death itself makes life more loving. Men come closest to their true selves in the sober moments of life, under the shadows of sorrow and loss.

In the affairs of life or of business, it is not intellect that tells so much as character, not brains so much as heart, not genius so much as self-control, patience, and discipline④, regulated⑤ by judgment.

I have always believed that the man who has begun to live more seriously within begins to live more simply without. In an age of extravagance⑥ and waste, I wish I could show to the world how few the real wants of humanity⑦ are.

To regret one's errors to the point of not repeating them is true repentance⑧. There is nothing noble in being superior⑨ to some other man. The true nobility is in being superior to your previous self.

词汇释义

①**tangled** ['tæŋgld] *adj.* 纠缠的；紊乱的；混乱的；杂乱的
②**yarn** [jɑːn] *n.* 纱，线；（尤指）毛线；故事；（旅行）逸事
③**bereavement** [bɪ'riːvmənt] *n.* 亲人丧亡，丧失亲人，丧亲之痛
④**discipline** ['dɪsəplɪn] *n.* 训练；纪律；自制力；行为准则
⑤**regulate** ['regjuleɪt] *v.* 控制；调节；管理
⑥**extravagance** [ɪk'strævəgəns] *n.* 奢侈（品）；浪费
⑦**humanity** [hjuː'mænəti] *n.* 人类；人性；人道；人文学科
⑧**repentance** [rɪ'pentəns] *n.* 悔悟；悔改；后悔；忏悔
⑨**superior** [suː'pɪəriə(r)] *adj.* 比……好的；优良的；更高级的

难句解析

1. Men come closest to their true selves in the sober moments of life, under the shadows of sorrow and loss.

译文 人在生命的庄严时刻，在哀痛和伤心的阴影之下，最接近真实的自我。

解析 "come close to..." 译为"靠近，接近……"；"under the shadows of..." 译为"在……阴影之下"。

2. In the affairs of life or of business, it is not intellect that tells so much as character, not brains so much as heart, not genius so much as self-control, patience, and discipline, regulated by judgment.

译文 在生活或事业中，性格比才智更能指导我们，心灵比头脑更能引导我们，而由判断而得的克制、耐心和教养比天分更能让我们受益。

解析 "in the affairs of" 译为"在……的事务中"；"it is not intellect that…"

是一个强调句型,"intellect"译为"智力"。

本句将心灵、头脑、克制、耐心、教养和天分等放在一起,使我们明白后天的能力和修炼更能促进我们个人的发展。

参考译文

真正的高贵

风平浪静的大海,每个人都是领航员。

但是,只有阳光而无阴影,只有欢乐而无痛苦,那就不是人生。以最幸福的人的生活为例——它是一团纠缠在一起的麻线。丧亲之痛和幸福祝愿彼此相接,让我们悲欢交替,甚至死亡本身也会使生命更加可亲。人在生命的庄严时刻,在哀痛和伤心的阴影之下,最接近真实的自我。

在生活或事业中,性格比才智更能指导我们,心灵比头脑更能引导我们,而由判断而得的克制、耐心和教养比天分更能让我们受益。

我始终相信,开始在内心生活得更严肃的人,也会在外表上开始生活得更朴素。在一个奢华浪费的年代,我希望能向世界表明,人类真正需要的东西是非常之微少的。

悔恨自己的错误,而且力求不再重蹈覆辙,这才是真正的悔悟。优于别人,并不高贵,真正的高贵应该是优于过去的自己。

读后写作

Some people think that in order to get true nobility, we have to compare ourselves to the ones in the past. What's your opinion about it?

We Are on a Journey
人在旅途
——Henry Van Dyke

读前导语

本篇文章作者亨利·凡·戴克（1852—1933），美国作家、教育家、演说家。

他在文中写道："无论你身在何处，也无论你是何人，此时此刻，有一件事于你我而言都是相同的，而且只要我们活着，这个共同点就存在。那就是，我们并非停留不前，而是人在旅途。"

美文欣赏

Wherever you are, and whoever you may be, there is one thing in which you and I are just alike, at this moment, and in all the moments of our existence[①]. We are not at rest; we are on a journey. Our life is a movement, a tendency[②], a steady, ceaseless[③] progress towards an unseen goal.

We are gaining something, or losing something, every day. Even when our position and our character seem to remain precisely[④] the same, they are changing. For the mere advance of time is a change. It is not the same thing to have a bare field in January and in July. The season makes the difference. The limitations that are childlike in the child are childish in the man. Everything that we do is a step in one direction or another. Even the failure to do something is in itself a deed. It sets us forward or backward. The action of the negative pole of a magnetic[⑤] needle is just as real as the action of the positive pole. To decline[⑥] is to accept — the other alternative[⑦].

Are you nearer to your port today than you were yesterday? Yes, you must be a little nearer to some port or other; for since your ship was first launched⑧ upon the sea of life, you have never been still for a single moment; the sea is too deep, you could not find an anchorage⑨ if you would; there can be no pause until you come into port.

词汇释义

①**existence** [ɪɡˈzɪstəns] *n.* 存在；生活（方式）
②**tendency** [ˈtendənsi] *n.* 倾向；趋势；偏好；极端势力
③**ceaseless** [ˈsiːsləs] *adj.* 不停的，无休止的，不断的
④**precisely** [prɪˈsaɪsli] *adv.* 精确地；恰好地；严谨地，严格地
⑤**magnetic** [mæɡˈnetɪk] *adj.* 有磁性的，有吸引力的；磁性的
⑥**decline** [dɪˈklaɪn] *v.* 减少；衰落；下降；衰退；婉拒
⑦**alternative** [ɔːlˈtɜːnətɪv] *n.* 可供选择的事物
⑧**launch** [lɔːntʃ] *v.* 开始从事；发起；上市；发射；猛扑向前
⑨**anchorage** [ˈæŋkərɪdʒ] *n.* 锚地，泊地；固定处

难句解析

1. Wherever you are, and whoever you may be, there is one thing in which you and I are just alike, at this moment, and in all the moments of our existence.

【译文】 无论你身在何处，也无论你是何人，此时此刻，有一件事于你我而言都是相同的，而且只要我们活着，这个共同点就存在。

【解析】 "Wherever you are, and whoever you may be" 引导的是让步状语从句；"be alike" 译为"和……相像"；"in all the moments of our existence" 译为"在我们生存的每个瞬间、时刻"。

2. Yes, you must be a little nearer to some port or other; for since your ship was first launched upon the sea of life, you have never been still for a single moment;...

【译文】 是的，你肯定离某个港口更近了。因为自从你的航船从生命的海洋上起航的那一刻开始，你没有哪一刻是静止的。

【解析】 "be a little nearer to..." 译为"更加接近……"；"for" 引导原因状语从句；"launch" 本义是指"发射"，此处译为"（船只等）起航、出发"。

参考译文

人在旅途

　　无论你身在何处，也无论你是何人，此时此刻，有一件事于你我而言都是相同的，而且只要我们活着，这个共同点就存在。那就是，我们并非停留不前，而是人在旅途。我们的生命是一种运动，一种趋势，是向一个看不见的目标无休止地奋进。

　　每天，我们都有所得，也有所失。即便我们的位置和角色看似与原来无异，但实际上也是时时变化的。因为时间的推移本身就是一种变化。对于同一片荒地来说，在一月和七月是截然不同的，季节造成了这种差异。能力的局限在孩子身上被视为天真烂漫，而在大人身上则是幼稚的表现。我们所做的每件事情都是朝着某个方向迈进了一步。即使是失败本身，也是有所得的，失败可以催人奋进，也可以让人一蹶不振。磁针负极的作用与正极的作用都是一样真实的。拒绝也是一种接受，只不过是另一种选择罢了。

　　你今天比昨天更接近你的港口了吗？是的，你肯定离某个港口更近了。因为自从你的航船从生命的海洋上起航的那一刻开始，你没有哪一刻是静止的。大海如此深邃，即便你想停泊，也找不到地方；只有当你驶入自己的港口时，你才能停止下来。

读后写作

　　Life is like a journey that can't be stopped. Life is like a journey that has many ports, some of which are very important. What is your important port? Please share it with us.

Work and Pleasure
工作和娱乐
——Winston Churchill

读前导语

本篇文章作者温斯顿·丘吉尔（1874—1965），英国政治家、历史学家、演说家、作家、记者，第61、63届英国首相。

他在文中写道："要想真正生活得幸福和平安，一个人至少应该有两三种业余爱好，而且必须是真正的爱好。到了晚年才开始说"我要培养这个或那个兴趣"是毫无用处的，这种尝试只会增加精神上的负担。在与自己日常工作无关的领域中，一个人可以获得渊博的知识，但却很难有所收益或得到放松。做自己喜欢的事是无益的，你得喜欢自己所做的事。"

美文欣赏

To be really happy and really safe, one ought to have at least two or three hobbies, and they must all be real. It is no use starting late in life to say: "I will take an interest in this or that." Such an attempt only aggravates[①] the strain of mental effort. A man may acquire great knowledge of topics unconnected with his daily work, and yet hardly get any benefit or relief. It is no use doing what you like; you have got to like what you do. Broadly speaking, human being may be divided into three classes: those who are toiled[②] to death, those who are worried to death, and those who are bored to death. It is no use offering the manual laborer[③], tired out with a hard week's sweat and effort, the chance of playing a game of football or baseball on Saturday afternoon. It is no use inviting the politician or the professional or business man, who has been working or worrying about serious things for six days, to work or worry about trifling④ things at the weekend.

It may also be said that rational⑤, industrious⑥, useful human beings are divided into two classes: first, those whose work is work and whose pleasure is pleasure; and secondly, those whose work and pleasure are one. Of these the former are the majority. They have their compensations⑦. The long hours in the office or the factory bring with them as their reward, not only the means of sustenance⑧, but a keen appetite⑨ for pleasure even in its simplest and most modest forms. But Fortune's favored children belong to the second class. Their life is a natural harmony. For them the working hours are never long enough. Each day is a holiday, and ordinary holidays when they come are grudged⑩ as enforced interruptions in an absorbing vacation. Yet to both classes the need of an alternative outlook, of a change of atmosphere, of a diversion⑪ of effort, is essential. Indeed, it may well be that those whose work is their pleasure are those who most need the means of banishing⑫ it at intervals⑬ from their minds.

词汇释义

①**aggravate** ['ægrəveɪt] *v.* 加重；使恶化；激怒，惹恼

②**toil** [tɔɪl] *v.* 长时间或辛苦地工作；艰难缓慢地移动；跋涉

③**laborer** ['leɪbərə(r)] *n.* 体力劳动者，工人

④**trifling** ['traɪflɪŋ] *adj.* 微不足道的；轻浮的；无聊的；懒散的

⑤**rational** ['ræʃnəl] *adj.* 神志清楚的；理性的；理智的；合理的

⑥**industrious** [ɪn'dʌstriəs] *adj.* 勤劳的，勤奋的；勤恳的，刻苦的

⑦**compensation** [ˌkɒmpen'seɪʃn] *n.* 补偿；报酬

⑧**sustenance** ['sʌstənəns] *n.* 食物，营养，养料

⑨**appetite** ['æpɪtaɪt] *n.* 胃口；食欲；强烈欲望

⑩**grudge** [grʌdʒ] *vt.* 怀恨；妒忌；吝惜；不情愿做

⑪**diversion** [daɪ'vɜːʃn] *n.* 转向，偏离；令人分心的事情

⑫**banish** ['bænɪʃ] *vt.* 放逐，驱逐；消除，排除

⑬**interval** ['ɪntəvl] *n.* 间隔；幕间休息；（数学）区间

难句解析

1. A man may acquire great knowledge of topics unconnected with his daily work, and yet hardly get any benefit or relief.

译文 在与自己日常工作无关的领域中,一个人可以获得渊博的知识,但却很难有所收益或得到放松。

解析 "unconnected with"在此处作后置定语,修饰之前的"great knowledge of topics";"hardly"译为"几乎不"。

2. Indeed, it may well be that those whose work is their pleasure are those who most need the means of banishing it at intervals from their minds.

译文 事实上,那些把工作看作娱乐的人可能是需要以某种方式将工作不时地驱赶出自己的大脑。

解析 本句中"whose"引导定语从句,修饰之前的"those";"who"也引导定语从句,修饰之前的"those";"banishing ... from"译为"把……驱赶走";"at intervals"译为"不时地"。

参考译文

工作和娱乐

要想真正生活得幸福和平安,一个人至少应该有两三种业余爱好,而且必须是真正的爱好。到了晚年才开始说"我要培养这个或那个兴趣"是毫无用处的,这种尝试只会增加精神上的负担。在与自己日常工作无关的领域中,一个人可以获得渊博的知识,但却很难有所收益或得到放松。做自己喜欢的事是无益的,你得喜欢自己所做的事。广而言之,人可以分为三个类别:劳累而死的人,忧虑而死的人和无聊而死的人。对于那些体力劳动者来说,一周辛苦的工作使他们精疲力竭,因此在周六下午给他们提供踢足球或者打棒球的机会是没有意义的。对于政界人士、专业人士或者商人来说,他们已经为棘手的事务操劳或者烦恼了六天,因此在周末请他们为琐事劳神同样毫无意义。

或者可以这么说,理智的、勤奋的、有用的人可以分为两类:对第一类人而言,工作就是工作,娱乐就是娱乐;对于第二类人而言,工作和娱乐是合二为一的。很大一部分人属于前者。他们可以得到相应的补偿。在办公室或工厂里长时间的工作，不仅带给他们维持生计的金钱，还带给他们一种渴求娱乐的强烈欲望，哪怕这种娱乐消遣是以最简单、最淳朴的方式进行的。而第二类人则是命运的宠儿。他们的生活自然而和谐。在他们看来，工作时间永远不够多，每天都是假期；而当正常的假日到来时，他们总会抱怨自己有趣的休假被强行中断。然而，有一些东西对于这两类人来说都十分必要，那就是变换一下视角，改变一下氛围，尝试做点不同的事情。事实上，那些把工作看作娱乐的人可能是需要以某种方式将工作不时地驱赶出自己的大脑。

读后写作

How to keep balance between work and pleasure? Do you have any good idea?

What is Your Recovery Rate?
你的恢复速率是多少？
——Graham Harris

读前导语

本篇文章作者格雷厄姆·哈里斯（1894—1976），证券分析师。他享有"华尔街教父"的美誉。代表作品有《证券分析》《聪明的投资者》等。

他在文中写道："沉湎过去，就无法与今天同行，明天因而也成了一个遥遥的无期。沉湎过去，就无法让我们每天过得精彩，痛苦因而就成了一个咒语无法摆脱。"

美文欣赏

What is your recovery rate? How long does it take you to recover from actions and behaviors that upset you? Minutes? Hours? Days? Weeks? The longer it takes you to recover, the more influence that incident① has on your actions, and the less able you are to perform to your personal best. In a nutshell②, the longer it takes you to recover, the weaker you are and the poorer your performance.

You are well aware that you need to exercise to keep the body fit and, no doubt, accept that a reasonable measure of health is the speed in which your heart and respiratory③ system recovers after exercise. Likewise the faster you let go of an issue that upsets you, the faster you return to an equilibrium④, the healthier you will be. The best example of this behavior is found with professional sportspeople. They know that the faster they can forget an incident or missed opportunity and get on with the game, the better their performance. In fact, most measure the time it takes them to overcome and

— 99 —

forget an incident in a game and most reckon⑤ a recovery rate of 30 seconds is too long!

Imagine yourself to be an actor in a play on the stage. Your aim is to play your part to the best of your ability. You have been given a script⑥ and at the end of each sentence is a full stop. Each time you get to the end of the sentence you start a new one and although the next sentence is related to the last it is not affected by it. Your job is to deliver each sentence to the best of your ability.

Don't live your life in the past! Learn to live in the present, to overcome the past. Stop the past from influencing your daily life. Don't allow thoughts of the past to reduce your personal best. Stop the past from interfering⑦ with your life. Learn to recover quickly.

Remember: Rome wasn't built in a day. Reflect on your recovery rate each day. Every day before you go to bed, look at your progress. Don't lie in bed saying to you, "I did that wrong." "I should have done better there." No. Look at your day and note when you made an effort to place a full stop after an incident. This is a success. You are taking control of your life. Remember this is a step by step process. This is not a make-over. You are undertaking real change here. Your aim: reduce the time spent in recovery.

Live in the present. Not in the precedent⑧.

词汇释义

①**incident** [ˈɪnsɪdənt] *n.* 事件，事变；小插曲；敌对行动；骚乱
②**nutshell** [ˈnʌtʃel] *n.* 坚果的外壳；简言之，一言以蔽之
③**respiratory** [rəˈspɪrətri] *adj.* 呼吸的
④**equilibrium** [ˌiːkwɪˈlɪbriəm] *n.* 平衡，均势；平静
⑤**reckon** [ˈrekən] *v.* 测算，估计；认为；计算；评定，断定
⑥**script** [skrɪpt] *n.* 脚本，手迹；书写体铅字；剧本、广播稿等
⑦**interfere** [ˌɪntəˈfɪə(r)] *v.* 干涉，妨碍
⑧**precedent** [ˈpresɪdənt] *n.* 前例；先例

难句解析

1. The longer it takes you to recover, the more influence that incident has on your

actions, and the less able you are to perform to your personal best.

[译文] 你需要的恢复时间越长,那个事件对你的影响就越大,你也就越不能做到最好。

[解析] "the longer it takes you to recover, the more influence..., and the less..." 使用的是"the more..., the more..."结构,译为"越……,越……",此句型在此处又出现了第三个比较级,对所描述的事物进行了更加详细的说明。

2. Each time you get to the end of the sentence you start a new one and although the next sentence is related to the last it is not affected by it.

[译文] 每次你念到一个句子的末尾,你就会开始一个新的句子。尽管下一句和上一句有关联,但并不受它的影响。

[解析] "each time"译为"每次",此处用作连词引导时间状语从句。"is related to"译为"和……相关"。

参考译文

你的恢复速率是多少?

你的恢复速率是多少?你需要多长时间才能从让你烦恼的行为中恢复?几分钟?几小时?几天?几星期?你需要的恢复时间越长,那个事件对你的影响就越大,你也就越不能做到最好。简言之,你的恢复时间越长,你就越软弱,你的表现也就越差劲。

你充分意识到,要保持身体健康你需要锻炼,并且你无疑会接受,你的心脏和呼吸系统在锻炼后的恢复速度是衡量健康的一个合理尺度。同样,你越快摆脱使你烦恼的问题,越快恢复平静,你就越健康。此类行为的最好典范是专业运动员。他们知道,越快忘记一件事或失去的机会而好好比赛,他们的发挥就越好。实际上,大多数运动员会估量自己克服并忘记比赛中一个事件所需的时间,而且大多数人都认为30秒的恢复时间太长了!

想象自己是一位站在舞台上的戏剧演员。你的目标是尽全力扮演好你的角色。你已经拿到了剧本,而剧本中的每句话都以句号结尾。每次你念到一个句子的末尾,你就会开始一个新的句子。尽管下一句和上一句有关联,但并不受它的影响。你的工作是尽力说好每句台词。

不要生活在过去!要学会生活在现在,学会克服过去;不要让过去影响你的日常生活；不要让过去的思想妨碍你做到最好；不要让过去干扰你的生活；学会快速恢复。

记住，罗马不是一日建成的。每天都反思自己的恢复速率；每天上床睡觉前，都看看自己的进步。不要躺在床上对自己说："我那个做错了。""我应该做得更好。"不要那样做。回想自己的一天，并注意努力给某个事件画上句号的时刻。这就是一种成功。你在控制自己的生活。记住这是一个循序渐进的过程，这不是简单的修修补补。你正在进行的是真正的改变，你的目标是减少用在恢复上的时间。

生活在现在，而不是从前。

读后写作

"Live in the present. Not in the precedent/past." Please share your understanding of the sentence by telling a story about it.

Be Happy!
活得快乐!
——Lloyd Morris

读前导语

本篇文章作者劳埃德·莫里斯(1613—1680),英国著名作家,作品富于机智幽默。著有《格言集》等。本文以演绎的手法论述快乐对人的影响。

他在文中写道:"积极的快乐并非单纯的满意或知足,通常不期而至,就像四月里突然下起的春雨,或是花蕾的突然绽放。然后,你就会发觉与快乐结伴而来的究竟是何种智慧。"

美文欣赏

"The days that make us happy make us wise." —John Masefield

When I first read this line by England's Poet Laureate, it startled me. What did Masefield mean? Without thinking about it much, I had always assumed that the opposite was true. But his sober assurance① was arresting②. I could not forget it.

Finally, I seemed to grasp his meaning and realized that here was a profound③ observation. The wisdom that happiness makes possible lies in clear perception④, not fogged by anxiety nor dimmed⑤ by despair and boredom, and without the blind spots caused by fear.

Active happiness—not mere satisfaction or contentment⑥—often comes suddenly, like an April shower or the unfolding of a bud. Then you discover what kind of wisdom has accompanied it. The grass is greener; bird songs are sweeter; the shortcomings of your friends are more understandable and more forgivable⑦. Happiness is like a pair of eyeglasses correcting your spiritual vision.

　　Nor are the insights of happiness limited to what is near around you. Unhappy, with your thoughts turned in upon your emotional woes⑧, your vision is cut short as though by a wall. Happy, the wall crumbles⑨.

　　The long vista is there for the seeing. The ground at your feet, the world about you—people, thoughts, emotions, pressures—are now fitted into the larger scene. Everything assumes a fairer proportion⑩. And here is the beginning of wisdom.

词汇释义

①**assurance** [ə'ʃʊərəns] *n.* 保证；自信

②**arrest** [ə'rest] *v.* 逮捕，拘留；阻止；吸引

③**profound** [prə'faʊnd] *adj.* 深厚的；意义深远的；知识渊博的

④**perception** [pə'sepʃn] *n.* 知觉；觉察（力）；观念

⑤**dim** [dɪm] *v.* （使）变昏暗，变模糊，变渺茫；（使）减弱

⑥**contentment** [kən'tentmənt] *n.* 满足，满意，知足，心满意足

⑦**forgivable** [fə'gɪvəbl] *adj.* 可宽恕的

⑧**woe** [wəʊ] *n.* 悲哀；悲伤；灾难，灾殃；苦恼

⑨**crumble** ['krʌmbl] *v.* （使）破碎；坍塌；崩溃；无力应付

⑩**proportion** [prə'pɔːʃn] *n.* 部分，份额；比例；重要性；均衡

难句解析

1. The wisdom that happiness makes possible lies in clear perception, not fogged by anxiety nor dimmed by despair and boredom, and without the blind spots caused by fear.

【译文】 快乐带来的睿智存在于敏锐的洞察力之间，不会因忧虑而含混迷惑，也不会因绝望和厌倦而黯然模糊，更不会因恐惧而造成盲点。

【解析】 "that" 引导定语从句，修饰之前的 "the wisdom"； "lie in" 译为

"在于"; 在 "not fogged by... nor dimmed by..." 中, "not... nor" 的用法和 "neither... nor..." 的用法类似, 译为 "既不……也不……"。

2. Unhappy, with your thoughts turned in upon your emotional woes, your vision is cut short as though by a wall. Happy, the wall crumbles.

译文 当你不快乐时,你的思维陷入情感上的悲哀,你的眼界就像是被一道墙给阻隔了,而当你快乐时,这道墙就会砰然倒塌。

解析 "with your thoughts turned in upon your emotional woes",此处使用的是 "with" 的复合结构,即 "with+宾语+宾语补足语" 的形式,在句中充当伴随状语。

参考译文

活得快乐

"快乐的日子使人睿智。"——约翰·梅斯菲尔德

第一次读到英国桂冠诗人梅斯菲尔德的这行诗时,我感到十分震惊。他想表达什么意思?我以前从未对此仔细考虑,总是认定这行诗反过来才正确。但他冷静而又胸有成竹的表达引起了我的关注,令我无法忘怀。

终于,我似乎领会了他的意思,并意识到这行诗意义深远。快乐带来的睿智存在于敏锐的洞察力之间,不会因忧虑而含混迷惑,也不会因绝望和厌倦而黯然模糊,更不会因恐惧而造成盲点。

积极的快乐并非单纯的满意或知足,通常不期而至,就像四月里突然下起的春雨,或是花蕾的突然绽放。然后,你就会发觉与快乐结伴而来的究竟是何种智慧。草地更为青翠,鸟吟更为甜美,朋友的缺点也变得更能让人理解、宽容。快乐就像一副眼镜,可以矫正你的精神视力。

快乐的视野并不仅限于你周围的事物。当你不快乐时,你的思维陷入情感上的悲哀,你的眼界就像是被一道墙给阻隔了,而当你快乐时,这道墙就会砰然倒塌。

你的眼界变得更为宽广。你脚下的大地,你身边的世界,包括人、思想、情感和压力,现在都融入了更为广阔的景象之中,其间每件事物的比例都更加合理。而这就是睿智的起始。

读后写作

What is happiness? A thousand people have a thousand answers. In fact, happiness is very simple, and it is just a perception in the heart of the individual. The less desire you have, the more satisfaction and happiness you will get. Please write a short paragraph to describe the happy moment you experience.

To Be or Not to Be
生存或者毁灭
——William Lyon Phelps

读前导语

本篇文章作者威廉·利昂·菲尔普斯（1865—1943），美国教育家、文学评论家和演说家，耶鲁大学教授与学者，兼任电台节目和报纸专栏的撰稿人，经常发表公众演讲，著作涉及小说理论研究等多方面，代表作有《现代小说家评论集》《20世纪戏剧》等，为普及文学教育做出了重要贡献。

他在文中写道："每当你有了一种新的兴趣——甚至是一种新的技艺——你就增加了自己生命的能量。一个对许多事物都深感兴趣的人不可能总不快乐，真正的悲观者是那些失去兴趣的人。"

美文欣赏

"To be or not to be." Outside the *Bible*, these six words are the most famous in all the literature of the world. They were spoken by Hamlet when he was thinking aloud, and they are the most famous words in Shakespeare because Hamlet was speaking not only for himself but also for every thinking man and woman. To be or not to be, to live or not to live, to live richly and abundantly and eagerly, or to live dully[①] and meanly and scarcely[②]. A philosopher once wanted to know whether he was alive or not, which is a good question for everyone to put to himself occasionally. He answered it by saying: "I think, therefore I am."

But the best definition of existence I ever saw was one written by another philosopher[③] who said: "To be is to be in relations." If this true, then the more

— 107 —

relations a living thing has, the more it is alive. To live abundantly④ means simply to increase the range and intensity of our relations. Unfortunately we are so constituted⑤ that we get to love our routine. But apart from our regular occupation how much are we alive? If you are interested only in your regular occupation, you are alive only to that extent. So far as other things are concerned—poetry and prose, music, pictures, sports, unselfish friendships, politics, international affairs—you are dead.

Contrariwise⑥, it is true that every time you acquire a new interest—even more, a new accomplishment—you increase your power of life. No one who is deeply interested in a large variety of subjects can remain unhappy; the real pessimist⑦ is the person who has lost interest.

Bacon said that a man dies as often as he loses a friend. But we gain new life by contacting with new friends. What is supremely⑧ true of living objects is only less true of ideas, which are also alive. Where your thoughts are, there will your life be also. If your thoughts are confined⑨ only to your business, only to your physical welfare, only to the narrow circle of the town in which you live, then you live in a narrow circumscribed⑩ life. But if you are interested in what is going on in China, then you are living in China; if you're interested in the characters of a good novel, then you are living with those highly interesting people; if you listen intently⑪ to fine music, you are away from your immediate surroundings and living in a world of passion and imagination.

To be or not to be—to live intensely and richly, merely to exist, that depends on ourselves. Let us widen and intensify⑫ our relations. While we live, let us live!

词汇释义

①**dully** [ˈdʌlli] *adv.* 迟钝地；沉闷地；呆滞地；乏味地

②**scarcely** [ˈskeəsli] *adv.* 几乎不，简直不；刚刚

③**philosopher** [fəˈlɒsəfə(r)] *n.* 哲学家，思想家；善于思考的人

④**abundantly** [əˈbʌndəntli] *adv.* 丰富地；大量地；十分清楚

⑤**constitute** [ˈkɒnstɪtjuːt] *v.* 组成，构成；被视为；设立

⑥**contrariwise** [kənˈtreərɪwaɪz] *adv.* 反之；顽固地

⑦**pessimist** [ˈpesɪmɪst] *n.* 悲观主义者，悲观者；厌世者

⑧**supremely** [suːˈpriːmli] *adv.* 极其，极度

⑨**confine** ［kənˈfaɪn］ *v.* 限制；监禁，关押
⑩**circumscribed** ［ˈsɜːkəmskraɪbd］ *adj.* 局限的；受限制的
⑪**intently** ［ɪnˈtentli］ *adv.* 专心地；专注地；热切地；热心地
⑫**intensify** ［ɪnˈtensɪfaɪ］ *v.* 增强，加剧

难句解析

1. They were spoken by Hamlet when he was thinking aloud, and they are the most famous words in Shakespeare because Hamlet was speaking not only for himself but also for every thinking man and woman.

［译文］ 这六个字是哈姆雷特喃喃自语时所说的，而这六个字也是莎士比亚作品中最有名的几个字，因为哈姆雷特不仅道出了自己的心声，也道出了所有在思考的人的心声。

［解析］ "when he was thinking aloud" 用法巧妙，用"thinking aloud"表示"在心中喃喃自语"；"not only ..., but also ..."表示"不但……，而且……"。

2. Contrariwise, it is true that every time you acquire a new interest—even more, a new accomplishment—you increase your power of life.

［译文］ 反之，每当你有了一种新的兴趣——甚至是一种新的技艺——你就增加了自己生命的能量。

［解析］ "contrariwise"译为"反之"；"it is true that"引导主语从句，之后的"every time"引导时间状语从句。

参考译文

生存或者毁灭

"生存还是毁灭。"除《圣经》以外，这六个字是整个世界文学中最著名的六个字。这六个字是哈姆雷特喃喃自语时所说的，而这六个字也是莎士比亚作品中最有名的几个字，因为哈姆雷特不仅道出了自己的心声，也道出了所有在思考的人的心声。生存还是毁灭——是活下去还是不要活下去，是要生活得丰富充实、兴致勃勃，还是生活得枯燥委琐、贫乏无味。一位哲人曾想弄清自己是否在活着，其实这个问题我们每个人都应该不时地扪心自问。他对这个问题的答案是："我思，故我在。"

但是我所见过的关于生存最好的定义却出自另一位哲学家："生活即是联系。"如果这句话不假，那么一个生物拥有的联系越多，它就越有活力。所谓要活得丰富也即是要扩大和加强我们的各种联系。不幸的是，我们天生就容易陷入自己的陈规旧套。试问除去我们的日常事务，我们在多大程度上是活着的？如果你只对日常事务感兴趣，那你的生命也就局限于那个范围之内。就其他事物而言——诗歌、散文、音乐、美术、体育、无私的友谊、政治、国际事务等等——你只是一个死人。

反之，每当你有了一种新的兴趣——甚至是一种新的技艺——你就增加了自己生命的能量。一个对许多事物都深感兴趣的人不可能总不快乐，真正的悲观者是那些失去兴趣的人。

培根曾说，一个人每当失去朋友便死一次，但是通过结交新朋友，我们就能获得新的生命。这个对于生物来说千真万确的道理也完全适用于人的思想，思想也是有生命的。你思想之所在即是你生命之所在。如果你的思想只局限于自己的工作、自己的物质利益、自己所居住的城镇内狭小的生活圈子，那么你的生命也是局限的、狭小的。但是如果你对当前中国所发生的种种事情感兴趣，那么你就相当于生活在那些极有趣的人中间；如果你能全神贯注地听绝妙的音乐，你就会超脱周围环境而生活在一个充满激情与想象的世界之中。

生存与毁灭——是活得热烈而丰富，还是活得像行尸走肉，那都取决于我们自己。让我们扩大并加强我们的联系吧。活着就要精彩！

读后写作

"To be or not to be", which is a question we have asked ourselves for many times. Actually we make decisions at every moment. Please write a short paragraph to describe the most important decision you have ever made.

27 On Beauty
论 美
——Kahlil Gibran

读前导语

本篇文章作者卡里·纪伯伦（1883—1931），被称为"艺术天才""黎巴嫩文坛骄子"，是阿拉伯文学的主要奠基人，20世纪阿拉伯新文学道路的开拓者之一。其主要作品有《泪与笑》《先知》《沙与沫》等，蕴含了丰富的社会性和东方精神，不以情节为重，旨在抒发丰富的情感。纪伯伦、鲁迅和泰戈尔一样是近代东方文学走向世界的先驱。他与印度的泰戈尔并称"站在东西方文化桥梁上的两位巨人"。

他在文中写道："美是生活揭开了她神圣的面纱。而你就是生活，就是面纱。美是凝视自己镜中之影的永恒。而你就是镜子，就是永恒。"

美文欣赏

Where shall you seek beauty, and how shall you find her unless she herself be your way and your guide? And how shall you speak of her except she be the weaver[①] of your speech?

The aggrieved[②] and the injured say, "Beauty is kind and gentle. Like a young mother half-shy of her own glory she walks among us."

And the passionate[③] say, "Nay, beauty is a thing of might and dread[④]. Like the tempest she shakes the earth beneath[⑤] us and the sky above us."

The tired and the weary say, "Beauty is of soft whisperings. She speaks in our spirit. Her voice yields to our silences like a faint light that quivers[⑥] in fear of the shadow."

But the restless say, "We have heard her shouting among the mountains. And with her cries came the sound of hoofs, and the beating of wings and the roaring of lions."

At night the watchmen of the city say, "Beauty shall rise with the dawn from the east." And at noontide the toilers and the wayfarers say, "We have seen her leaning over the earth from the windows of the sunset."

In winter say the snow-bound, "She shall come with the spring leaping upon the hill."

And in the summer heat the reapers say, "We have seen her dancing with the autumn leaves, and we saw a drift of snow in her hair."

All these things have you said of beauty. Yet in truth you spoke not of her but of needs unsatisfied, and beauty is not a need but an ecstasy⑦. It is not a mouth thirsting nor an empty hand stretched⑧ forth, but rather a heart enflamed⑨ and a soul enchanted. It is not the image you would see nor the song you would hear, but rather an image you see though you close your eyes and a song you hear though you shut your ears. It is not the sap⑩ within the furrowed⑪ bark, nor a wing attached to a claw⑫, but rather a garden forever in bloom and a flock of angels forever in flight.

Beauty is life when life unveils⑬ her holy face.

But you are life and you are the veil.

Beauty is eternity⑭ gazing at itself in a mirror.

But you are eternity and you are the mirror.

词汇释义

①**weaver** ['wiːvə(r)] *n.* 织工，编织者；织巢鸟，织网蜘蛛

②**aggrieved** [ə'griːvd] *adj.* 愤愤不平的，受委屈的；悲痛的

③**passionate** ['pæʃənət] *adj.* 热烈的；激昂的；易怒的

④**dread** [dred] *n.* 恐惧，令人恐惧的事物

⑤**beneath** [bɪ'niːθ] *prep.* 在……下面；在……背后；比不上

⑥**quiver** ['kwɪvə(r)] *v.* 微颤，抖动

⑦**ecstasy** ['ekstəsi] *n.* 狂喜；出神，忘形；无法自控的情绪

⑧**stretch** [stretʃ] *v.* 伸展；拉紧；绵延，延续

⑨**enflame** ［ɪnˈfleɪm］ *v.* 燃烧

⑩**sap** ［sæp］ *n.* 精力，元气；树液；活力；坑道

⑪**furrow** ［ˈfʌrəʊ］ *v.* 犁田，开沟；使起皱纹

⑫**claw** ［klɔː］ *n.* 爪；螯，钳

⑬**unveil** ［ˌʌnˈveɪl］ *vt.* 揭去……的面罩；使公之于众；揭露

⑭**eternity** ［ɪˈtɜːnəti］ *n.* 永恒；永生，不朽；极长的一段时间

难句解析

1. Where shall you seek beauty, and how shall you find her unless she herself be your way and your guide?

［译文］ 如果美不以自身为途径，为向导，你们到哪里，又如何找到她呢？

［解析］ "unless" 引导条件状语从句，表示"除非；如果不……"；"be one's way" 此处可理解为"成为某人的道路"，与之后的"guide"一词相呼应。

2. Yet in truth you spoke not of her but of needs unsatisfied, and beauty is not a need but an ecstasy.

［译文］ 然而事实上，人们说的不是美，而是未得到满足的需求，而美不是一种需求，是一种狂喜。

［解析］ "speak of" 在此处译为"谈及，谈论到"；"not ... but ..." 译为"不是……而是……"。

参考译文

论 美

如果美不以自身为途径，为向导，你们到哪里，又如何找到她呢？如果她不是你们言语的编织者，你们又如何谈论她呢？

受委屈、受伤害的人说："美是仁慈和温柔，就像一位年轻妈妈，因自己的光荣而半带羞涩地走在我们中间。"

富有激情的人说："不，美是一种强大而可畏的东西，就像惊天动地的暴风雨。"

劳累疲倦的人说："美是柔声细语。她在我们的心灵中窃窃私语。她的声音沉浸在我们的寂静中，正如一抹光在阴影的恐惧中颤抖。"

但是焦躁不安的人说:"我们听见美在山中的呼喊。随着她的呼喊,我们听到了走兽嗒嗒的蹄声,鸟儿噼啪的振翅声和群狮的咆哮声。"

夜晚,城市的巡夜人说:"美将伴随着晨曦从东方升起。"正午时分,干苦力的人和徒步旅行的人说:"我们看见美倚在黄昏之窗眺望大地。"

冬天,为大雪所困的人说:"美随着春天在小山上跳跃。"

在炎炎夏日,收庄稼的人说:"我们看见她伴着秋叶跳舞,看见她的头发里雪花飞扬。"

关于美,人们众说纷纭。然而事实上,人们说的不是美,而是未得到满足的需求,而美不是一种需求,是一种狂喜。不是干渴的嘴唇和伸出的空手,而是滚烫的心和愉悦的灵魂;不是你想看的样子和想听的东西,而是虽闭上眼睛也能看到的模样,虽掩住耳朵也能听到的旋律;不是褶皱树皮下的汁液,不是利爪下的鸟儿,而是花开四季的园林,是翱翔天空的天使。

美是生活揭开了她神圣的面纱。

而你就是生活,就是面纱。

美是凝视自己镜中之影的永恒。

而你就是镜子,就是永恒。

读后写作

Everyone has a love for beauty. Which do you think is more impressive, a beautiful appearance or a beautiful mind? Show your opinion here.

Summer Sunrises on the Mississippi
密西西比河上夏天的日出
——Mark Twain

读前导语

本篇文章作者马克·吐温（1835—1910），美国作家、演说家。代表作品有小说《百万英镑》《哈克贝利·费恩历险记》《汤姆·索亚历险记》等。

他在文中写道："一切都是那么美；或淡雅，或浓郁，无一不美；太阳高高升起时，从此处看，它的周围泛着粉红色的晕圈，从彼处看，它又洒着一粒粒的金光，最妙不可言的，是它周围若隐若现的紫色。"

美文欣赏

One can never see too many summer sunrises on the Mississippi. They are enchanting[①]. First, there is the eloquence[②] of silence; for a deep hush broods[③] everywhere. Next, there is the haunting[④] sense of loneliness, isolation, remoteness from the worry and bustle[⑤] of the world. The dawn creeps in stealthily[⑥]; the solid walls of the black forest soften to grey, and vast stretches of the river open up and reveal[⑦] themselves; the water is smooth, gives off spectral[⑧] little wreaths of white-mist, there is not the faintest breath of wind, nor stir of leaf; the tranquility[⑨] is profound and infinitely satisfying. Then a bird pipes up, another follows, and soon the pipings develop into a jubilant[⑩] riot[⑪] of music. You see none of the birds, you simply move through an atmosphere of song which seems to sing itself. When the light has become a little stronger, you have one of the fairest and softest pictures imaginable. You have the intense green of the massed and crowded foliage[⑫] nearby; you see it paling[⑬] shade by shade in front of you; upon the next projecting cape, a mile off or more, the tint has lightened to the tender young green of spring; the cape beyond that one has almost lost colour, and the furthest one, miles away under the horizon, sleeps upon the water a mere dim vapour⑭, and hardly separable⑮ from the sky above it and about it. And all this stretch of river is a mirror, and you have shadowy reflections of the leafage⑯ and the curving shores and the receding⑰ capes pictured in it.

Well, this is all beautiful; soft and rich and beautiful; and when the sun gets well up, and distributes a pink flush here and a powder of gold yonder and a purple haze where it will yield the best effect, you grant⑱ that you have something that is worth remembering.

词汇释义

① **enchanting** [ɪnˈtʃɑːntɪŋ] *adj.* 使人喜悦的；妩媚的；迷人的

② **eloquence** [ˈeləkwəns] *n.* 辩才；文采

③ **brood** [bruːd] *n.* （雏鸡、鸟等的）一窝；一家的孩子

④ **haunting** [ˈhɔːntɪŋ] *adj.* 萦绕心头的；不易忘怀的

⑤ **bustle** [ˈbʌsl] *n.* 喧闹

⑥ **stealthily** [ˈstelθɪli] *adv.* 暗地里，偷偷摸摸地；秘密地

⑦ **reveal** [rɪˈviːl] *v.* 揭示；展示

⑧ **spectral** [ˈspektrəl] *adj.* （似）鬼的；幽灵的；谱的；光谱的

⑨ **tranquility** [træŋˈkwɪləti] *n.* 平静；安静；安宁；平稳

⑩ **jubilant** [ˈdʒuːbɪlənt] *adj.* 喜气洋洋的；欢呼的；喜庆的

⑪ **riot** [ˈraɪət] *n.* 混乱；五色缤纷

⑫ **foliage** [ˈfəʊliɪdʒ] *n.* 植物的叶子（总称），叶子及梗和枝；树叶

⑬ **pale** [peɪl] *v.* （颜色）变淡，变浅；使褪色

⑭ **vapour** [ˈveɪpə(r)] *n.* 潮气，水汽；蒸汽

⑮ **separable** [ˈsepərəbl] *adj.* 可分离的，可分的

⑯ **leafage** [ˈliːfɪdʒ] *n.* 叶子（总称），叶状装饰，树饰；叶丛

⑰ **recede** [rɪˈsiːd] *v.* 逐渐远离；向后倾斜

⑱ **grant** [ɡrɑːnt] *v.* 授予；承认；给予

难句解析

1. Next, there is the haunting sense of loneliness, isolation, remoteness from the worry and bustle of the world.

译文 随后，孤寂、隔绝的气息弥漫四周，丝毫没有尘世的烦恼与喧嚣。

解析 "the haunting sense of ..." 译为 "……萦绕心头的感觉"；用 "loneliness, isolation, remoteness" 三个词语和 "worry and bustle" 形成对比，凸显美景。

2. Then a bird pipes up, another follows, and soon the pipings develop into a jubilant riot of music. You see none of the birds, you simply move through an atmosphere of song which seems to sing itself.

译文 接着，一只鸟儿叫出声来，其他鸟儿也陆续鸣叫，很快，鸟儿们的叫声俨然变成一首欢快的歌曲。但你丝毫见不着它们的身影；你只感觉动听的歌声如天籁般从四处传来。

解析 "pipe up" 此处译为 "叫出声来"；"simply" 译为 "仅仅，只"；"which" 引导定语从句，修饰之前的 "an atmosphere of song"，在从句中充当主语。

参考译文

密西西比河上夏天的日出

夏天，密西西比河上的日出奇美无比，令人百看不厌。日出伊始，河面一片宁静，仿佛世界都陷入了沉思当中。随后，孤寂、隔绝的气息弥漫四周，丝毫没有尘世的烦恼与喧嚣。跟着黎明悄然而至；那一片黑压压的森林，如城垣一般坚不可摧，也缓缓地被日光融化成灰色，广阔的水域也渐渐清晰，映入眼帘；河水如玻璃一般明净，在光谱的映照下泛出一圈一圈的白晕，河面上风平浪静，落叶仿佛也受到感染，纹丝不动；一切是如此地静谧，如此地赏心悦目！接着，一只鸟儿叫出声来，其他鸟儿也陆续鸣叫，很快，鸟儿们的叫声俨然变成一首欢快的歌曲。但你丝毫见不着它们的身影；你只感觉动听的歌声如天籁般从四处传来。当光线稍微变强时，一切如梦如幻，柔和淡雅，美不胜收。河的附近，树木枝繁叶茂，郁郁葱葱；放眼望去，一排厚似一排，直至暗无踪影；沿着河岸走一英里左右，来到下一个河岬，这周围的色调比之前稍淡，宛似春天的翠绿色；再前一处的河岬更淡，若有似无，最远的那个河岬，低于地平线数尺，朦朦胧胧，依稀可见，仿佛枕在水面上，与天相接，不分彼此。广阔的河面好似一面明镜，淡淡地映照着丛集的枝叶、蜿蜒的河岸和渐行渐远的河岬。

一切都是那么美；或淡雅，或浓郁，无一不美；当太阳高高升起时，从此处看，它的周围泛着粉红色的晕圈，从彼处看，它又洒着一粒粒的金光，最妙不可言的，是它周围若隐若现的紫色。这一切，能不令人怀想？

读后写作

Have you ever enjoyed some beautiful scenery? Please write a short paragraph to tell us the most impressive one.

Choice of Companions
择 友
——William Thackeray

读前导语

本文作者威廉·萨克雷（1811—1863），英国作家。

他在文中写道："一位好友胜于一笔财富，因为财富买不来朋友身上的珍贵品德，而正是这些品德使人们之间的交往成为一件幸事。最好的朋友就是比我们更睿智、更出色的人，我们可以被他的智慧和美德所激励，从而使我们的行为更加高尚。"

美文欣赏

A good companion[①] is better than a fortune[②], for a fortune cannot purchase those elements of character which make companionship a blessing. The best companion is one who is wiser and better than ourselves, for we are inspired by his wisdom and virtue to nobler deeds. Greater wisdom and goodness than we possess lifts us higher mentally and morally.

It is true that we cannot always choose all of our companions. Some are thrust[③] upon us by business and the social relations of life. We do not choose them, we do not enjoy them, and yet we have to associate with them more or less. The experience is not altogether without compensation[④], if there be principle enough in us to bear the strain. Still, in the main, choice of companions can be made, and must be made. It is not best or necessary for a young person to associate with "Tom, Dick and Henry" without forethought[⑤] or purpose. Some fixed rules about the company he or she keeps should be observed. The subject should be uppermost[⑥] in the thoughts, and canvassed[⑦] often.

Companionship is education, good or bad; it develops manhood or womanhood, high or low, it lifts the soul upward or drags it downward; it ministers[8] to virtue or vice[9]. There is no half way work about its influence. If it ennobles[10], it does it grandly. If it demoralizes[11], it does it devilishly, it saves or destroys lustily[12]. Nothing in the world is surer than this. Sow virtue, and the harvest will be virtue. Sow vice, and the harvest will be vice. Good companions help us to sow virtue; evil companions help us to sow vice.

词汇释义

①**companion** [kəmˈpænjən] *n.* 同伴；陪伴；陪护

②**fortune** [ˈfɔːtʃuːn] *n.* 大笔的钱；时运，运气；命运

③**thrust** [θrʌst] *v.* 猛推；逼迫；强行推入；延伸

④**compensation** [ˌkɒmpenˈseɪʃn] *n.* 补偿/赔偿金；补偿；报酬

⑤**forethought** [ˈfɔːθɔːt] *n.* 事先的考虑；远见卓识

⑥**uppermost** [ˈʌpəməʊst] *adj.* 最高的；至上的；最重要的

⑦**canvass** [ˈkænvəs] *v.* 游说；征求意见；详细检查

⑧**minister** [ˈmɪnɪstə(r)] *v.* 满足（……的需要）；帮助

⑨**vice** [vaɪs] *n.* 罪行；恶行，邪恶；缺点；老虎钳

⑩**ennoble** [ɪˈnəʊbl] *vt.* 封……为贵族，使高贵

⑪**demoralize** [dɪˈmɒrəlaɪz] *vt.* 使士气低落；使陷入混乱

⑫**lustily** [ˈlʌstɪli] *adv.* 精力充沛地；强壮地

难句解析

1. A good companion is better than a fortune, for a fortune cannot purchase those elements of character which make companionship a blessing.

[译文] 一位好友胜于一笔财富，因为财富买不来朋友身上的珍贵品德，而正是这些品德使人们之间的交往成为一件幸事。

[解析] 此处使用比较级"is better than"来表示朋友对于一个人来说胜过一笔财富，"for"引导原因状语从句；"which"引导定语从句，在从句中充当主语，修饰之前的"those elements of character"。

2. Still, in the main, choice of companions can be made, and must be made. It is not best or necessary for a young person to associate with "Tom, Dick and Henry" without forethought or purpose.

译文 但总的来说，朋友可以选择，也必须选择。如果没有事先的掂量或明确的目的，一个年轻人就随便与张三、李四或王五交往，那是不妥当的，也是不必要的。

解析 "It is not best or necessary for a young person to…"使用的结构是"It is +adj. for sb. to do sth."；"associate with"译为"与……交往"。

参考译文

择 友

　　一位好友胜于一笔财富，因为财富买不来朋友身上的珍贵品德，而正是这些品德使人们之间的交往成为一件幸事。最好的朋友就是比我们更睿智、更出色的人，我们可以被他的智慧和美德所激励，从而使我们的行为更加高尚。他们有着比我们更多的智慧和更高尚的情操，从而促使我们不断提高自己的精神境界和道德水平。

　　不可否认的是，有些朋友总是我们无法选择的。有些人是由于生意和各种社会关系的缘故被硬塞给我们的。我们没有选择他们，我们也不喜欢他们，但是我们必须或多或少地跟他们交往。如果我们坚守内心的原则，承受一些压力，这样的经历并非完全没有补偿。但总的来说，朋友可以选择，也必须选择。如果没有事先的掂量或明确的目的，一个年轻人就随便与张三、李四或王五交往，那是不妥当的，也是不必要的。需要注意的是，结交朋友时必须确立一些原则。这一点务必在思想上引起重视，并时时自查。

　　无论益友还是损友，都会使我们受到教育。无论对男还是对女，它都可以滋养高尚或卑微的人格，它可以使灵魂升华，也可以使之堕落。它可以滋生美德，也可以催生邪恶。它的影响没有折中之道。友谊，如果使人高尚，就会使人如天使般庄重。如果使人堕落，就会使人如魔鬼般邪恶。它可以有力地拯救一个人，也可以轻易地毁掉一个人。世上没有什么事比这更确定无疑了。播种美德，收获的就是美德。播种邪恶，收获的就是邪恶。好的朋友可以帮助我们播种美德，坏的朋友促使我们播种邪恶。

> 读后写作

The key to happiness is having a confidant or a group of friends. Social connections can help us live healthier lives and withstand more stress. Therefore, maintaining a healthy and long-lasting friendship is worth the effort. Can you introduce one of your best friends to us?

When Love Beckons You
爱的召唤
——Kahlil Gibran

读前导语

本篇文章作者卡里·纪伯伦（1883—1931），黎巴嫩的文坛骄子，诗人、杰出作家，他和泰戈尔一样都是近代东方文学走向世界的先驱，是"站在东西方文化桥梁上的巨人"。他的代表作有《泪与笑》《先知》《沙与沫》《叛逆的灵魂》和《折断的翅膀》等，其主要作品蕴含了丰富的社会性和东方精神，不以情节为重，旨在抒发丰富的情感。

他在文中写道："爱会给你戴上桂冠，也会折磨你。爱会助你成长，也会给你修枝。爱会上升到枝头，抚爱你在阳光下颤动的嫩枝，也会下潜至根部，撼动你紧抓泥土的根基。"

美文欣赏

When love beckons① to you, follow him, though his ways are hard and steep. And when his wings enfold② you, yield③ to him, though the sword hidden among his pinions④ may wound you. And when he speaks to you, believe in him, though his voice may shatter⑤ your dreams as the north wind lays waste the garden.

For even as love crowns you so shall he crucify⑥ you. Even as he is for your growth so is he for your pruning⑦. Even as he ascends⑧ to your height and caresses your tenderest branches that quiver⑨ in the sun, so shall he descend⑩ to our roots and shake them in their clinging⑪ to the earth.

But if, in your fear, you would seek only love's peace and love's pleasure, then it

— 123 —

is better for you that you cover your nakedness and pass out of love's threshing-floor, into the seasonless⑫ world where you shall laugh, but not all of your laughter, and weep, but not all of your tears. Love gives naught but itself and takes naught but from itself. Love possesses not, nor would it be possessed, for love is sufficient⑬ unto love.

Love has no other desire but to fulfill⑭ itself. But if you love and must have desires, let these be your desires:

To melt and be like a running brook that sings its melody to the night.

To know the pain of too much tenderness⑮.

To be wounded by your own understanding of love;

And to bleed willingly and joyfully.

To wake at dawn with a winged heart and give thanks for another day of loving;

To rest at the noon hour and meditate⑯ love's ecstasy;

To return home at eventide⑰ with gratitude;

And then to sleep with a payer for the beloved in your heart and a song of praise upon your lips.

词汇释义

①**beckon** ['bekən] *v.* 招手示意；吸引；很可能发生

②**enfold** [ɪn'fəʊld] *v.* 围住；抱紧

③**yield** [jiːld] *v.* 产生；屈服，让步；放弃；让路

④**pinion** ['pɪnjən] *n.* 鸟翼

⑤**shatter** ['ʃætə(r)] *vt.* 使破碎，使碎裂，砸碎

⑥**crucify** ['kruːsɪfaɪ] *vt.* 折磨，虐待

⑦**prune** [pruːn] *v.* 删除；减少

⑧**ascend** [ə'send] *v.* 上升，登高；升职

⑨**quiver** ['kwɪvə(r)] *v.* 微颤，抖动

⑩**descend** [dɪ'send] *v.* 下来，下降，下斜；沦落；降临

⑪**cling** [klɪŋ] *v.* 附着于；抓紧或抱住；坚持；依恋，依附于

⑫**seasonless** ['siːznləs] *adj.* 不分季节的

⑬**sufficient** [sə'fɪʃnt] *adj.* 足够的；充足的；充分的

⑭**fulfill** [fʊl'fɪl] *vt.* 履行；执行（命令等）；达到（目的）

⑮**tenderness** ['tendənəs] *n.* 柔软；温和；亲切；心软难处理

⑯**meditate** ['medɪteɪt] *v.* 沉思；打算

⑰**eventide** ['iːvntaɪd] *n.* 黄昏，日暮

难句解析

1. And when his wings enfold you, yield to him, though the sword hidden among his pinions may wound you.

[译文] 当爱的羽翼拥抱你时，请顺从他，尽管隐藏在其羽翼之下的剑可能会伤到你。

[解析] "enfold"译为"拥抱"；"yield to"译为"顺从"；"hidden"一词作后置定语，修饰之前的"the sword"。

2. But if, in your fear, you would seek only love's peace and love's pleasure, then it is better for you that you cover your nakedness and pass out of love's threshing-floor, into the seasonless world where you shall laugh, but not all of your laughter, and weep, but not all of your tears.

[译文] 但是，如果你在恐惧之中只想寻求爱的平和与快乐，那你就最好掩盖真实的自我，避开爱的考验，进入不分季节的世界，在那里你将欢笑，但并非开怀大笑，你将哭泣，但并非尽情地哭。

[解析] "it is better for you that …"使用的是"it is +*adj.* + for sb. + that …"的句型；"cover your nakedness"译为"掩盖最本真的自我"；"where"引导定语从句，修饰之前的"the seasonless world"，在从句中充当状语成分。

参考译文

爱的召唤

当爱召唤你时，请追随他，尽管爱的道路艰难险峻。当爱的羽翼拥抱你时，请顺从他，尽管隐藏在其羽翼之下的剑可能会伤到你。当爱向你诉说时，请相信他，尽管他的声音可能打破你的梦想，就如同北风吹落花园里所有的花瓣。

爱会给你戴上桂冠，也会折磨你。爱会助你成长，也会给你修枝。爱会上升到枝头，抚爱你在阳光下颤动的嫩枝，也会下潜至根部，撼动你紧抓泥

土的根基。

但是，如果你在恐惧之中只想寻求爱的平和与快乐，那你最好掩盖真实的自我，避开爱的考验，进入不分季节的世界，在那里你将欢笑，但并非开怀大笑，你将哭泣，但并非尽情地哭。爱只将自己付出，也只得到自己。爱一无所有，也不会为谁所有，因为爱本身就已自足。

爱除了实现自我别无他求。但是如果你爱而又不得不有所求，那就请期望：

将自己融化并像奔流的溪水一般向夜晚吟唱自己优美的曲调。

明了过多的温柔所带来的苦痛。

被自己对爱的理解所伤害；

并情愿快乐地悲伤。

在黎明带着轻快的心醒来并感谢又一个有爱的日子；

在午休时沉思爱的心醉神怡；

在黄昏怀着感恩之心回家；

然后为内心所爱之人祈祷，吟唱赞美之歌，并带着祷告和歌声入眠。

读后写作

Love is an eternal theme. Please share the stories about love you heard or you experienced.

On Meeting the Celebrated
论见名人
——W. S. Maugham

读前导语

本篇文章的作者威廉·萨默塞特·毛姆（1874—1965），英国小说家、剧作家。代表作有戏剧《圈子》，长篇小说《人生的枷锁》《月亮和六便士》，短篇小说《叶的震撼》《阿金》等。

他在文中写道："大人物经常是千人一面，小人物身上才有一组组矛盾元素，是取之不尽的创作源泉，让你惊喜不断。"

美文欣赏

I have always wondered at the passion many people have to meet the celebrated①. The prestige② you acquire by being able to tell your friends that you know famous men proves only that you are yourself of small account③. The celebrated develop a technique to deal with the persons they come across. They show the world a mask, often an impressive on, but take care to conceal④ their real selves. They play the part that is expected from them, and with practice learn to play it very well, but you are stupid if you think that this public performance of theirs corresponds⑤ with the man within.

I have been attached, deeply attached, to a few people; but I have been interested in men in general not for their own sakes, but for the sake of my work. I have not, as Kant enjoined, regarded each man as an end in himself, but as material that might be useful to me as a writer. I have been more concerned with the obscure⑥ than with the famous. They are more often themselves. They have had no need to create a figure to protect themselves from the world or to impress it. Their idiosyncrasies[7] have had more chance to develop in the limited circle of their activity, and since they have never been in the public eye it has never occurred to them that they have anything to conceal. They display their oddities[8] because it has never struck them that they are odd. And after all it is with the common run of men that we writers have to deal; kings, dictators, commercial magnates are from our point of view very unsatisfactory. To write about them is a venture that has often tempted[9] writers, but the failure that has attended their efforts shows that such beings are too exceptional to form a proper ground for a work of art. They cannot be made real. The ordinary is the writer's richer field. Its unexpectedness, its singularity[10], its infinite variety afford unending material. The great man is too often all of a piece; it is the little man that is a bundle[11] of contradictory elements. He is inexhaustible[12]. You never come to the end of the surprises he has in store for you. For my part I would much sooner spend a month on a desert island with a veterinary[13] surgeon than with a prime minister.

词汇释义

① **celebrated** [ˈselɪbreɪtɪd] *adj.* 有名的，著名的

② **prestige** [preˈstiːʒ] *n.* 威信，威望，声望；声誉

③ **account** [əˈkaʊnt] *n.* 账号；账目，账单；赊购；描述，解释

④ **conceal** [kənˈsiːl] *v.* 隐藏；隐瞒，掩饰；遮住

⑤ **correspond** [ˌkɒrəˈspɒnd] *v.* 符合；相当于；通信

⑥ **obscure** [əbˈskjʊə(r)] *adj.* 昏暗的，朦胧的；隐蔽的；无名的

⑦ **idiosyncrasy** [ˌɪdiəˈsɪŋkrəsi] *n.* （某人特有的）气质，习性

⑧ **oddity** [ˈɒdəti] *n.* 奇特，奇异；怪癖；怪人，怪事

⑨ **tempt** [tempt] *vt.* 引诱，怂恿；吸引；冒……的风险；使感兴趣

⑩ **singularity** [ˌsɪŋɡjuˈlærəti] *n.* 异常；奇怪；奇特；奇点

⑪ **bundle** [ˈbʌndl] *n.* 捆，包；一批

⑫ **inexhaustible** [ˌɪnɪɡˈzɔːstəbl] *adj.* 无穷无尽的，用不完的

⑬ **veterinary** [ˈvetnri] *adj.* 兽医的

难句解析

1. I have been attached, deeply attached, to a few people; but I have been interested in men in general not for their own sakes, but for the sake of my work.

译文 我自己就喜欢一些人，非常喜欢他们。但我对人感兴趣一般不是因为他们自身的缘故，而是出于我的工作需求。

解析 "be attached to" 译为 "爱慕，喜欢"；"for the sake of" 译为 "以……的名义"；"not ... but ..." 表示 "不是……而是……"。

2. For my part I would much sooner spend a month on a desert island with a veterinary surgeon than with a prime minister.

译文 就我而言，如果在孤岛上度过一个月，我宁愿和一名兽医相守，也不愿同一位首相做伴。

解析 "spend" 译为 "度过"；"would much sooner ... than ..." 译为 "宁愿……也不……"。

参考译文

论见名人

许多人热衷于见名人，我始终不得其解。在朋友面前吹嘘自己认识某某名人，由此而来的声望只能证明自己的微不足道。名人个个练就了一套处世高招儿，无论遇上谁，都能应付自如。他们给世人展现的是一副面具，常常是美好难忘的面具，但他们会小心翼翼地掩盖自己的真相。他们扮演的是大家期待的角色，演得多了，最后都能演得惟妙惟肖。如果你还以为他们在公众面前的表演就是他们的真实自我，那你就傻了。

我自己就喜欢一些人，非常喜欢他们。但我对人感兴趣一般不是因为他们自身的缘故，而是出于我的工作需求。正如康德劝告的那样，我从来没有把认识某人作为目的，而是将其当作对一个作家有用的创作素材。比之名流显士，我更加关注无名小卒。他们常常显得较为自然真实，他们无须再创造另一个人物形象，用他来保护自己不受世人干扰，或者用他来感动世人。他们的社交圈子有限，自己的种种癖性也就越有可能得到滋长。因为他们从来没有引起公众的关注，也就从来没有想到过要隐瞒什么。他们会表露他们古怪的一面，因为他们从来就没有觉得有何古怪。总之，作家要写的是普通人。在我们看来，国王、独裁者和商界大亨等都是不符合条件的。去撰写这些人物经常是作家们难以抗拒的冒险之举，可为此付出的努力不免以失败告终，这说明这些人物都过于特殊，无法成为一件艺术作品的创作根基，作家也不可能把他们写得真真切切。老百姓才是作家的创作沃土，他们或变幻无常，或难觅其二，各式人物应有尽有，这些都给作家提供了无限的创作素材。大人物经常是千人一面，小人物身上才有一组组矛盾元素，是取之不尽的创作源泉，让你惊喜不断。就我而言，如果在孤岛上度过一个月，我宁愿和一名兽医相守，也不愿同一位首相做伴。

读后写作

Do you agree with the author in the passage? What is your opinion about meeting the celebrated?

The Faculty of Delight
喜悦的力量
——Charles Edward Montague

读前导语

本篇文章作者查尔斯·爱德华·蒙塔古（1867—1928），英国作家。

他在文中写道："在人的心理能力中，有一种是很多孩子和艺术家自然就有的。不论是谁，一旦有了这种能力，直到他生命的最后一天也不一定会丢失。这就是从某一事物，或任一事物，都能感受到快乐的能力。"

美文欣赏

Among the mind's powers is one that comes of itself to many children and artists. It need not be lost, to the end of his days, by any one who has ever had it. This is the power of taking delight in a thing, or rather in anything, everything, not as a means to some other end, but just because it is what it is, as the lover dotes[①] on whatever may be the traits[②] of the beloved[③] object. A child in the full health of his mind will put his hand flat on the summer turf, feel it, and give a little shiver of private glee[④] at the elastic[⑤] firmness of the globe. He is not thinking how well it will do for some game or to feed sheep upon. That would be the way of the wooer[⑥] whose mind runs on his mistress's money. The child's is sheer affection, the true ecstatic[⑦] sense of the thing's inherent characteristics. No matter what the things may be, no matter what they are good or no good for, there they are, each with a thrilling[⑧] unique look and feel of its own, like a face; the painted wood familiarly[⑨] warmer, the clod crumbling[⑩] enchantingly[⑪] down in the hands, with its little dry smell of the sun and of hot nettles; each common thing a personality marked by delicious differences.

The joy of an Adam new to the garden and just looking round is brought by the normal child to the things that he does as well as those that he sees. To be suffered to do some plain work with the real spade⑫ used by mankind can give him a mystical⑬ exaltation⑭; to come home with his legs, as the French say, reentering his body from the fatigue of helping the gardener to weed beds sends him to sleep in the glow of a beatitude⑮ that is an end in itself...

The right education, if we could find it, would work up this creative faculty of delight into all its branching possibilities of knowledge, wisdom, and nobility. Of all three it is the beginning, condition, or raw material.

词汇释义

①**dote** [dəʊt] *v.* 溺爱，宠爱，过分地喜爱
②**trait** [treɪt] *n.* 特点，特征，特性
③**beloved** [bɪˈlʌvd] *adj.* 深爱的；钟爱的
④**glee** [gliː] *n.* 快乐，欢喜；重唱的歌曲
⑤**elastic** [ɪˈlæstɪk] *adj.* 有弹性的；灵活的
⑥**wooer** [ˈwuːə(r)] *n.* 求爱者
⑦**ecstatic** [ɪkˈstætɪk] *adj.* 狂喜的；入迷的，出神的
⑧**thrilling** [ˈθrɪlɪŋ] *adj.* 令人兴奋的；毛骨悚然的
⑨**familiarly** [fəˈmɪliəli] *adv.* 亲密地；精通地
⑩**crumble** [ˈkrʌmbl] *v.* （使）破碎；坍塌；崩溃；无力应付
⑪**enchantingly** [ɪnˈtʃɑːntɪŋli] *adv.* 使人喜悦地；妩媚地
⑫**spade** [speɪd] *n.* 铁锹，铲子；（纸牌中的）黑桃
⑬**mystical** [ˈmɪstɪkl] *adj.* 神秘的，奥秘的
⑭**exaltation** [ˌegzɔːlˈteɪʃn] *n.* 兴奋，得意扬扬
⑮**beatitude** [bɪˈætɪˌtjuːd] *n.* 至福；祝福

难句解析

1. This is the power of taking delight in a thing, or rather in anything, everything,

not as a means to some other end, but just because it is what it is, as the lover dotes on whatever may be the traits of the beloved object.

【译文】 这就是从某一事物，或任一事物，都能感受到快乐的能力，不是为了某一目的，只是因为它就是这样，这好比一个人喜爱一样东西，不论它有什么特征他都喜爱。

【解析】 "take delight in" 译为"从……获得快乐"；第一个"as"在此处译为"作为，当作"；第二个"as"译为"像……一样，如同"；"dote on"译为"溺爱，宠爱"。

2. The right education, if we could find it, would work up this creative faculty of delight into all its branching possibilities of knowledge, wisdom, and nobility.

【译文】 正确的教育，如果我们能够发现它，可以调动这一带有创造性的快乐的天赋，使其纳入所有可能的各个方面——知识、智慧和高尚的情操。

【解析】 "if we could find it" 在此处是插入语；"work up" 在此处译为"调动"；"branching possibilities of knowledge" 中的"branching"用法非常巧妙。

参考译文

喜悦的力量

在人的心理能力中，有一种是很多孩子和艺术家自然就有的。不论是谁，一旦有了这种能力，直到他生命的最后一天也不一定会丢失。这就是从某一事物，或任一事物，都能感受到快乐的能力，不是为了某一目的，只是因为它就是这样，这好比一个人喜爱一样东西，不论它有什么特征他都喜爱。一个心理健全的孩子会把他的手掌平放在夏天的草皮上，抚摸它，在他感觉到具有弹性又很坚实的地球表面时，他心里便产生一种快乐的冲动。他不是在想要是在上面做游戏或放羊什么的该有多好哇。那岂不是就像求婚者一心只想着女友的钱财一样吗？而孩子则完全是因为喜爱，是事物内在的特质真正让他有一种欣喜若狂的感觉。不论是什么事物，也不论它们有没有用途，它们就在那里，每一样东西都像一张脸孔，都有其独特的使人激动的面容和感觉；上过油漆的木器则让人感觉温和而亲切，当土块在手里松动而散发出阳光和热荨麻的微干的气味时，简直让人陶醉；每一样普通的东西都有它自己的"性格"，而这"性格"都有其不同的怡人的特征。

一个像亚当那样的人初次来到花园举目四望时所感到的那种快乐，一个正常孩子在其所做及所见的事物里都可以感觉到。在他被允许使用人类常用的铁锹去做一些简单的体力劳动时，他会感到一种神奇的兴奋；由于帮助园丁在花坛里锄草已经很疲劳，回到家时，就像法国人常说的那样，他的双腿又重新回到他的身上，在一种幸福的光辉里进入梦乡，这本身就是目的……

正确的教育，如果我们能够发现它，可以调动这一带有创造性的快乐的天赋，使其纳入所有可能的各个方面——知识、智慧和高尚的情操。对于这三者，这种心理能力是开始，是条件，或是原始材料。

读后写作

We all have the right to choose. Choosing to be happy is the best choice, which has a lot of benefits in our life. Please share one of the most happy moments with us.

Part II
Wonderful Celebrity Speeches
第二部分　名人演讲精彩瞬间

Gettysburg Address
葛底斯堡演说
—— Abraham Lincoln

读前导语

　　本篇文章作者亚伯拉罕·林肯（1809—1865），美国政治家、战略家、第 16 任总统。林肯是首位共和党籍总统，在任期间主导废除了美国黑人奴隶制。

　　本篇文章作为总统发表的最著名的演讲，也是美国历史上为人引用最多之演说，发表于美国南北战争期间。演讲只用了两分钟的时间，全文一共只有 10 句话，不到 300 个字，但字字珠玑，令人动情。1863 年 11 月 19 日，林肯总统在宾夕法尼亚州的葛底斯堡国家公墓揭幕式中发表此次演说，哀悼在长达五个半月的葛底斯堡之役中阵亡的将士。

美文欣赏

　　Four score① and seven years ago, our fathers brought forth upon this continent②, a new nation, conceived③ in Liberty and dedicated④ to the proposition that all men are created equal.

　　Now, we are engaged⑤ in a great civil war, testing whether that nation or any nation so conceived and so dedicated⑥, can long endure. We are met on a great battlefield of that war. We have come to dedicate a portion⑦ of that field as a final resting place for those who here gave their lives that that nation might live. It is altogether fitting and proper that we should do this.

　　But, in a larger sense, we cannot dedicate, we cannot consecrate⑧, we cannot hallow⑨ this ground. The brave men, living and dead, who struggled here, have consecrated it, far above our poor power to add or detract.

The world will little note, nor long remember what we say here, but it can never forget what they did here. It is for us, the living, rather, to be dedicated here to the unfinished work which they who fought here have thus far so nobly advanced. It is rather for us to be here dedicated to the great task remaining before us—that from these honored dead we take increased devotion to that cause for which they gave the last full measure of devotion; that we here highly resolve that these dead shall not have died in vain; that this nation, under God, shall have a new birth of freedom; and that government of the people, by the people, and for the people, shall not perish⑩ from the earth.

词汇释义

①**score** [skɔː(r)] *n.* 二十

②**continent** [ˈkɒntɪnənt] *n.* 大陆；欧洲大陆

③**conceive** [kənˈsiːv] *v.* 想象，构想；认为

④**dedicate** [ˈdedɪkeɪt] *v.* 献身于，致力于；题献词

⑤**engaged** [ɪnˈɡeɪdʒd] *adj.* 忙碌的

⑥**dedicated** [ˈdedɪkeɪtɪd] *adj.* 专注的，投入的；献身的；专用的

⑦**portion** [ˈpɔːʃn] *n.* 一部分；分得的财产

⑧**consecrate** [ˈkɒnsɪkreɪt] *vt.* 奉献，献祭

⑨**hallow** [ˈhæləʊ] *vt.* 使成为神圣，把……视为神圣

⑩**perish** [ˈperɪʃ] *v.* 毁灭；腐烂，枯萎；老化

难句解析

1. Fourscore and seven years ago, our fathers brought forth upon this continent, a new nation, conceived in Liberty and dedicated to the proposition that all men are created equal.

[译文] 八十七年以前，我们的祖先在这块大陆上创立了一个孕育于自由的

新国家，他们主张人人生而平等，并为此而献身。

[解析] "fathers"译为"祖先，先辈"；"bring forth upon"译为"带来"；"conceived in Liberty"译为"孕育于自由之中"；"dedicated to the proposition"译为"为此而奋斗、献身"，之后的that引导的是同位语从句，从句解释说明主张内容"人人生而平等"。

2. It is for us, the living, rather, to be dedicated here to the unfinished work which they who fought here have thus far so nobly advanced.

[译文] 相反地，我们活着的人，应该献身于勇士们未竟的工作，那些曾在此战斗过的人们已经把这项工作英勇地向前推进了。

[解析] "the living"是指"活着的人"，此处充当"us"的同位语，明确了我们的身份；"It is for us, the living, rather, to be dedicated here to …"使用的是"It is for sb. to do sth."的结构；"the unfinished work which they who fought here have thus far so nobly advanced"中的"which"引导定语从句，修饰之前的"the unfinished work"，在从句中充当"advance"的宾语，"who"引导定语从句，修饰之前的"they"，在从句中充当主语。

参考译文

葛底斯堡演说

八十七年以前，我们的祖先在这块大陆上创立了一个孕育于自由的新国家，他们主张人人生而平等，并为此而献身。

现在我们正进行一场伟大的内战，这是一场检验这一国家或者任何一个像我们这样孕育于自由并信守其主张的国家是否能长久存在的战争。我们聚集在这场战争中一个伟大战场上，将这个战场上的一块土地奉献给那些在此地为了这个国家的生存而牺牲了自己生命的人，作为他们的最终安息之所。我们这样做是完全适当和正确的。

可是，从更广的意义上说，我们并不能奉献这块土地，我们不能使之神圣，我们也不能使之光荣。那些在此地奋战过的勇士们，不论是还活着的或是已死去的，已经使这块土地神圣了，远非我们微薄的力量所能予以增减的。

世人将不大会注意，更不会长久记住我们在这里所说的话，然而，他们将永远不会忘记这些勇士们在这里所做的事。相反地，我们活着的人，应该献身于勇士们未竟的工作，那些曾在此战斗过的人们已经把这项工作英勇地向前推进了。我们应该献身于留在我们面前的伟大任务，由于他们的光荣牺牲，我们会更加献身于他们为之奉献了最后一切的事业，我们要下定决心使那些死去的人不致白白牺牲，我们要使这个国家在上帝的庇佑下，获得自由的新生，我们要使这个民有、民治、民享的政府不致从地球上消失。

读后写作

You must have learned something about Abraham Lincoln after reading *Gettysburg Address*. Please find some information about him and write a short passage to introduce him.

I Have a Dream (Excerpts)
我有一个梦想（节选）
—— Martin Luther King JR

读前导语

本篇文章是马丁·路德·金（1929—1968）最著名的演讲稿。他是非裔美国人，出生于美国佐治亚州亚特兰大，美国牧师、社会活动家、民权主义者，美国民权运动领袖。1963 年 8 月 28 日，在林肯纪念堂前，他发表了《我有一个梦想》的演说。他是 1964 年诺贝尔和平奖的获得者。马丁·路德·金被美国的权威期刊《大西洋月刊》评为影响美国的 100 位人物第 8 名。

他在文中写道："我梦想有一天，幽谷上升，高山下降，坎坷曲折之路成坦途，圣光披露，满照人间。"

美文欣赏

Five score years ago, a great American, in whose symbolic shadow we stand today, signed the Emancipation Proclamation. This momentous[①] decree came as a great beacon light of hope to millions of Negro slaves who had been seared in the flames of withering[②] injustice. It came as a joyous daybreak to end the long night of bad captivity.

But one hundred years later, the Negro still is not free. One hundred years later, the life of the Negro is still sadly crippled[③] by the manacles of segregation[④] and the chains of discrimination. One hundred years later, the Negro lives on a lonely island of poverty in the midst of a vast ocean of material prosperity. One hundred years later, the Negro is still languished[⑤] in the corners of American society and finds himself an exile[⑥] in his own land. So we've come here today to dramatize a shameful condition.

I am not unmindful that some of you have come here out of great trials and tribulations. Some of you have come fresh from narrow jail cells. Some of you have come from areas where your quest for freedom left you battered by the storms of persecution[7] and staggered by the winds of police brutality[8]. You have been the veterans[9] of creative suffering. Continue to work with the faith that unearned suffering is redemptive.

Go back to Mississippi, go back to Alabama, go back to South Carolina, go back to Georgia, go back to Louisiana, go back to the slums and ghettos[10] of our northern cities, knowing that somehow this situation can and will be changed. Let us not wallow[11] in the valley of despair.

I say to you today, my friends, so even though we face the difficulties of today and tomorrow, I still have a dream. It is a dream deeply rooted in the American dream.

I have a dream that one day this nation will rise up, live up to the true meaning of its creed: "We hold these truths to be self-evident; that all men are created equal."

I have a dream that one day on the red hills of Georgia the sons of former slaves and the sons of former slave-owners will be able to sit down together at the table of brotherhood.

I have a dream that one day even the state of Mississippi, a state sweltering[12] with the heat of injustice, sweltering with the heat of oppression, will be transformed into an oasis of freedom and justice.

I have a dream that my four children will one day live in a nation where they will not be judged by the color of their skin but by the content of their character.

I have a dream today.

I have a dream that one day down in Alabama with its governor having his lips dripping with the words of interposition[13] and nullification[14], one day right down in Alabama little black boys and black girls will be able to join hands with little white boys and white girls as sisters and brothers.

I have a dream today.

I have a dream that one day every valley shall be exalted[15], every hill and mountain shall be made low, the rough places will be made plain, and the crooked[16] places will be made straight, and the glory of the Lord shall be revealed, and all flesh shall see it together.

This is our hope. This is the faith that I go back to the South with. With this faith we will be able to hew out of the mountain of despair a stone of hope. With this faith we will be able to transform the jangling discords of our nation into a beautiful symphony of brotherhood. With this faith we will be able to work together, to pray together, to struggle together, to go to jail together, to stand up for freedom together, knowing that we will be free one day.

This will be the day when all of God's children will be able to sing with new meaning.

My country, 'tis of thee,

Sweet land of liberty,

Of thee I sing:

Land where my fathers died,

Land of the pilgrims' pride,

From every mountainside,

Let freedom ring.

And if America is to be a great nation this must become true.

So let freedom ring from the prodigious hilltops of New Hampshire.

Let freedom ring from the mighty mountains of New York!

Let freedom ring from the heightening Alleghenies of Pennsylvania!

Let freedom ring from the snowcapped[17] Rockies of Colorado!

Let freedom ring from the curvaceous slops of California!

But not only that; let freedom ring from Stone Mountain of Georgia!

Let freedom ring from Lookout Mountain of Tennessee!

Let freedom ring from every hill and molehill of Mississippi!

From every mountainside, let freedom ring!

When we let freedom ring, when we let it ring from every village and every hamlet, from every state and every city, we will be able to speed up that day when all of God's children, black men and white men, Jews and Gentiles, Protestants and Catholics, will be able to join hands and sing in the words of the old Negro spiritual, "Free at last! Free at last! Thank God almighty, we are free at last!"

词汇释义

①**momentous** [məˈmentəs] *adj.* 重大的；重要的

②**wither** [ˈwɪðə(r)] v. （使）枯萎，凋谢；破灭

③**cripple** [ˈkrɪpl] v. 使残疾；严重损坏，严重削弱

④**segregation** [ˌsegrɪˈɡeɪʃn] n. 分离，隔离；种族隔离

⑤**languish** [ˈlæŋɡwɪʃ] vi. 憔悴，潦倒

⑥**exile** [ˈeksaɪl] n. 流放，流亡；被流放者

⑦**persecution** [ˌpɜːsɪˈkjuːʃn] n. 迫害，残害；烦扰；苛求

⑧**brutality** [bruːˈtæləti] n. 野蛮行径，残暴行为

⑨**veteran** [ˈvetərən] n. 经验丰富的人，老兵

⑩**ghetto** [ˈɡetəʊ] n. 少数民族的集中住宅区；限制区，分离区

⑪**wallow** [ˈwɒləʊ] vi. 沉迷；打滚；在海浪中颠簸

⑫**swelter** [ˈsweltə(r)] v. 热得难受

⑬**interposition** [ˌɪntəpəˈzɪʃən] n. 提出（异议）行为；插嘴（插入）行为；提出（异议）的事；插嘴（插入）的事

⑭**nullification** [ˌnʌlɪfɪˈkeɪʃən] n. 无效，废弃；取消

⑮**exalt** [ɪɡˈzɔːlt] vt. 提高，提升；赞扬；使得意；加强

⑯**crooked** [ˈkrʊkɪd] adj. 弯曲的；不正当的；歪扭的

⑰**snowcapped** [ˈsnəʊˌkæpt] adj. 顶部被雪所盖着的

难句解析

1. This momentous decree came as a great beacon light of hope to millions of Negro slaves who had been seared in the flames of withering injustice.

译文 这一庄严宣言犹如灯塔的光芒，给千百万在那摧残生命的不义之火中受煎熬的黑奴带来了希望。

解析 本句将"this momentous decree"比作"a great beacon light of hope"，以此说明林肯总统的《葛底斯堡演说》在美国历史上的重大意义；"who"引导定语从句，修饰之前的"millions of Negro slaves"，在从句中充当主语。

2. One hundred years later, the life of the Negro is still sadly crippled by the manacles of segregation and the chains of discrimination.

译文 然而一百年后的今天，黑人还没有得到自由，一百年后的今天，在种族隔离的镣铐和种族歧视的枷锁下，黑人的生活备受压榨。

【解析】 "is crippled by" 译为"被严重压榨/剥削";"the manacles of segregation" 和 "the chains of discrimination" 形成呼应,说明美国黑人奴隶的悲惨生活和命运。

3. I am not unmindful that some of you have come here out of great trials and tribulations. Some of you have come fresh from narrow jail cells. Some of you have come from areas where your quest for freedom left you battered by the storms of persecution and staggered by the winds of police brutality.

【译文】 我并非没有注意到,参加今天集会的人中,有些受尽苦难和折磨,有些刚刚走出窄小的牢房,有些由于寻求自由,曾在居住地惨遭疯狂迫害的打击,并在警察暴行的旋风中摇摇欲坠。

【解析】 "I am not unmindful that..." 引导表语从句。这部分排比句式的使用,增强了演讲中的气势,用 "great trials and tribulations" "narrow jail cells" "battered by the storms of persecution and staggered by the winds of police brutality" 等词汇描绘出美国黑人遭受的不公平、不公正的对待。

4. I have a dream that one day even the state of Mississippi, a state sweltering with the heat of injustice, sweltering with the heat of oppression, will be transformed into an oasis of freedom and justice.

【译文】 我梦想有一天,甚至连密西西比州这个正义匿迹、压迫成风、如同沙漠般的地方,也将变成自由和正义的绿洲。

【解析】 "that" 引导同位语从句,解释说明之前的 "dream" 一词,表达演讲者内心对于公平、公正、自由的呼唤和期待。本篇演讲稿多次使用 "I have a dream that..." 句型使得演讲气势恢宏,能引起广大听众的强烈共鸣。

参考译文

我有一个梦想(节选)

一百年前,一个伟大的美国人签署了解放黑奴宣言,今天我们就是在他的雕像前集会。这一庄严宣言犹如灯塔的光芒,给千百万在那摧残生命的不义之火中受煎熬的黑奴带来了希望。它的到来犹如欢乐的黎明,结束了束缚黑人的漫漫长夜。

然而一百年后的今天,黑人还没有得到自由,一百年后的今天,在种族隔离的镣铐和种族歧视的枷锁下，黑人的生活备受压榨。一百年后的今天，黑人仍生活在物质充裕的海洋中一个贫困的孤岛上。一百年后的今天，黑人仍然畏缩在美国社会的角落里，并且意识到自己是故土家园中的流亡者。今天我们在这里集会，就是要把这种骇人听闻的情况公之于众。

我并非没有注意到，参加今天集会的人中，有些受尽苦难和折磨，有些刚刚走出窄小的牢房，有些由于寻求自由，曾在居住地惨遭疯狂迫害的打击，并在警察暴行的旋风中摇摇欲坠。你们是人为痛苦的长期受难者。坚持下去吧，要坚决相信，忍受不应得的痛苦是一种赎罪。

让我们回到密西西比去，回到阿拉巴马去，回到南卡罗来纳去，回到佐治亚去，回到路易斯安那去，回到我们北方城市中的贫民区和少数民族居住区去，要心中有数，这种状况是能够也必将改变的。我们不要陷入绝望而不能自拔。

朋友们，今天我对你们说，在此时此刻，我们虽然遭受种种困难和挫折，我仍然有一个梦想。这个梦是深深扎根于美国的梦想中的。

我梦想有一天，这个国家会站立起来，真正实现其信条的真谛："我们认为这些真理是不言而喻的；人人生而平等。"

我梦想有一天，在佐治亚的红山上，昔日奴隶的儿子将能够和昔日奴隶主的儿子坐在一起，共叙兄弟情谊。

我梦想有一天，甚至连密西西比州这个正义匿迹、压迫成风、如同沙漠般的地方，也将变成自由和正义的绿洲。

我梦想有一天，我的四个孩子将在一个不是以他们的肤色，而是以他们的品格优劣来评判他们的国度里生活。

我今天有一个梦想。

我梦想有一天，阿拉巴马州能够有所转变，尽管该州州长现在仍然满口异议，反对联邦法令，但有朝一日，那里的黑人男孩和女孩将能够与白人男孩和女孩情同骨肉，携手并进。

我今天有一个梦想。

我梦想有一天，幽谷上升，高山下降，坎坷曲折之路成坦途，圣光披露，满照人间。

这就是我们的希望。我怀着这种信念回到南方。有了这个信念，我们将能从绝望之岭劈出一块希望之石。有了这个信念，我们将能把这个国家刺耳的争吵声，改变成为一支洋溢手足之情的优美交响曲。有了这个信念，我们将能一起工作，一起祈祷，一起斗争，一起坐牢，一起维护自由；因为我们知道，终有一天，我们是会自由的。

在自由到来的那一天，上帝的所有儿女们将以新的含义高唱这首歌。

我的祖国，

美丽的自由之乡，

我为您歌唱，

您是父辈逝去的地方，

您是最初移民的骄傲，

让自由之声，

响彻每个山冈。

如果美国要成为一个伟大的国家，这个梦想必须实现。

让自由的钟声从新罕布什尔州的巍峨峰巅响起来！

让自由的钟声从纽约州的崇山峻岭响起来！

让自由的钟声从宾夕法尼亚州阿勒格尼山的顶峰响起来！

让自由的钟声从科罗拉多州冰雪覆盖的落基山响起来！

让自由的钟声从加利福尼亚州蜿蜒的群峰响起来！

不仅如此，还要让自由的钟声从佐治亚州的石岭响起来！

让自由的钟声从田纳西州的瞭望山响起来！

让自由的钟声从密西西比州的每一座丘陵响起来！

让自由的钟声从每一片山坡响起来。

当我们让自由钟声响起来，让自由钟声从每一个大小村庄、每一个州和每一个城市响起来时，我们将能够加速这一天的到来，那时，上帝的所有儿女，黑人和白人，犹太人和非犹太人，新教徒和天主教徒，都将手携手，合唱一首古老的黑人灵歌："终于自由啦！终于自由啦！感谢全能的上帝，我们终于自由啦！"

读后写作

Compared with Martin Luther King JR's dream, our dream is not that fabulous and fantastic. But we can have our own dreams. Please share one of your dreams with us.

First Inaugural Address of John F. Kennedy
(Excerpts)
肯尼迪总统就职演说（节选）
—— John F. Kennedy

读前导语

　　本篇文章作者约翰·肯尼迪（1917—1963），出生于美国马萨诸塞州布鲁克林，爱尔兰裔美国政治家。1960年，他当选为美国第35任总统。

　　本文就是他的就职演说。肯尼迪是美国历史上最年轻的总统，他的当选代表了二战后的年轻主张，肯尼迪的就职演说被认为是美国总统就职演说中最为精彩的篇章之一，其语言简明、结构巧妙，内容也反映了当时的政治、文化、社会背景，值得我们探究学习。

美文欣赏

　　We observe① today not a victory of party, but a celebration of freedom, symbolizing② an end, as well as a beginning; signifying renewal, as well as change. For I have sworn③ before you and Almighty God the same solemn④ oath⑤ our forebears prescribed⑥ nearly a century and three quarters ago.

　　In your hands, my fellow citizens, more than in mine, will rest the final success or failure of our course. Since this country was founded, each generation of Americans has been summoned⑦ to give testimony⑧ to its national loyalty⑨. The graves of young Americans who answered the call to service surround the globe.

Now the trumpet⑩ summons us again, not as a call to bear arms, though arms we need; not as a call to battle, though embattled we are; but a call to bear the burden of a long twilight struggle, year in and year out, "rejoicing⑪ in hope; patient in tribulation⑫", a struggle against the common enemies of man: tyranny⑬, poverty, disease, and war itself.

Can we forge against these enemies a grand and global alliance⑭, North and South, East and West, that can assure a more fruitful life for all mankind? Will you join in that historic effort?

In the long history of the world, only a few generations have been granted the role of defending freedom in its hour of maximum danger. I do not shrink⑮ from this responsibility. I welcome it. I do not believe that any of us would exchange places with any other people or any other generation. The energy, the faith, the devotion which we bring to this endeavor⑯ will light our country and all who serve it. And the glow from that fire can truly light the world.

And so, my fellow Americans, ask not what your country can do for you, ask what you can do for your country.

My fellow citizens of the world, ask not what America will do for you, but what together we can do for the freedom of man.

Finally, whether you are citizens of America or citizens of the world, ask of us here the same high standards of strength and sacrifice⑰ which we ask of you. With a good conscience our only sure reward, with history the final judge of our deeds, let us go forth to lead the land we love, asking His blessing and His help, but knowing that here on earth, God's work must truly be our own.

词汇释义

①**observe** [əbˈzɜːv] *v.* 庆祝

②**symbolize** [ˈsɪmbəlaɪz] *v.* 象征

③**sworn** [swɔːn] *v.* (swear 的过去分词) 就……宣誓；郑重承诺

④**solemn** [ˈsɒləm] *adj.* 严肃的；郑重的；庄严的

⑤**oath** [əʊθ] *n.* 誓言，誓约

⑥**prescribe** [prɪˈskraɪb] *vt.* 规定；指定

⑦**summon** [ˈsʌmən] *vt.* 召唤；召见；紧急寻求；传唤

⑧**testimony** [ˈtestɪməni] *n.* 证词；证言；声明；宣言

⑨**loyalty** [ˈlɔɪəlti] *n.* 忠诚，忠实；忠心

⑩**trumpet** [ˈtrʌmpɪt] *n.* 喇叭；号角

⑪**rejoice** [rɪˈdʒɔɪs] *v.* 非常高兴，深感欣喜

⑫**tribulation** [ˌtrɪbjuˈleɪʃn] *n.* 苦难；磨难；苦恼

⑬**tyranny** [ˈtɪrəni] *n.* 暴虐；专横；暴行

⑭**alliance** [əˈlaɪəns] *n.* 结盟；同盟；（尤指军事的）盟约

⑮**shrink** [ʃrɪŋk] *v.* 收缩；畏缩

⑯**endeavor** [ɪnˈdevə(r)] *n.* 努力；尽力

⑰**sacrifice** [ˈsækrɪfaɪs] *n.* 牺牲；舍身；献身

难句解析

1. We observe today not a victory of party, but a celebration of freedom, symbolizing an end, as well as a beginning; signifying renewal, as well as change.

译文 今天我们庆祝的不是政党的胜利，而是自由的胜利。这象征着一个结束，也象征着一个开端；意味着延续，也意味着变革。

解析 "observe"在此处是"庆祝"的意思；"not a victory of party, but a celebration of freedom"中的"not ... but..."译为"不是……而是……"；"as well as"在此处翻译成"也，和"。

2. "... but a call to bear the burden of a long twilight struggle, year in and year out, "rejoicing in hope; patient in tribulation", a struggle against the common enemies of man: tyranny, poverty, disease, and war itself.

译文 它召唤我们为迎接黎明而肩负起漫长斗争的重任，年复一年，从希望中得到欢乐，在磨难中保持耐性，对付人类共同的敌人——专制、贫穷、疾病

和战争本身。

【解析】 "a call to bear the burden" 中的 "call" 译为 "召唤，号召"，"bear" 在这里译为 "肩负"；"rejoicing in hope; patient in tribulation" 译为 "从希望中得到欢乐，在磨难中保持耐性"；"the common enemies of man" 中的 "man" 译为 "人类"。

参考译文

肯尼迪总统就职演说（节选）

今天我们庆祝的不是政党的胜利，而是自由的胜利。这象征着一个结束，也象征着一个开端；意味着延续，也意味着变革。因为我已在你们和全能的上帝面前，宣读了我们的先辈在170多年前拟定的庄严誓言。

公民们，我们方针的最终成败与其说掌握在我手中，不如说掌握在你们手中。自从合众国建立以来，每一代美国人都曾受到召唤去证明他们对国家的忠诚。响应召唤而献身的美国青年的坟墓遍及全球。

现在，号角已再次吹响——不是召唤我们拿起武器，虽然我们需要武器；不是召唤我们去作战，虽然我们严阵以待。它召唤我们为迎接黎明而肩负起漫长斗争的重任，年复一年，从希望中得到欢乐，在磨难中保持耐性，对付人类共同的敌人——专制、贫穷、疾病和战争本身。

为反对这些敌人，确保人类更为丰裕的生活，我们能够组成一个包括东西南北各方的全球大联盟吗？你们愿意参加这一历史性的努力吗？

在漫长的世界历史中，只有少数几代人在自由处于最危急的时刻被赋予保卫自由的责任。我不会推卸这一责任，我欢迎这一责任。我不相信我们中间有人想同其他人或其他时代的人交换位置。我们为这一努力所奉献的精力、信念和忠诚，将照亮我们的国家和所有为国效劳的人，而这火焰发出的光芒定能照亮全世界。

因此，美国同胞们，不要问国家能为你们做些什么，而要问你们能为国家做些什么。

全世界的公民们，不要问美国将为你们做些什么，而要问我们共同能为人类的自由做些什么。

最后，不论你们是美国公民还是其他国家的公民，你们应要求我们献出我们同样要求于你们的高度力量和牺牲。问心无愧是我们唯一可靠的奖赏，历史是我们行动的最终裁判，让我们走向前去，引导我们所热爱的国家。我们祈求上帝的福佑和帮助，但我们知道，确切地说，上帝在尘世的工作必定是我们自己的工作。

读后写作

John F. Kennedy is one of the greatest presidents in the history of the USA. Can you say something about him and his achievement?

First Inaugural Address of Franklin D. Roosevelt
罗斯福总统就职演说
—— Franklin D. Roosevelt

读前导语

　　本篇文章作者富兰克林·德拉诺·罗斯福（1882—1945），被称为"小罗斯福"，美国第 32 任总统，美国历史上首位连任四届的总统。罗斯福是第二次世界大战期间反法西斯同盟阵营的领导人之一，也是美国历史上在任时间最长的总统，他所发起的一些计划现在仍在美国的商贸中扮演重要角色，其任内设立的一些制度仍被保留。他曾多次被评为美国最佳总统。

　　本文就是他的就职演说。1933 年，民主党人罗斯福当选总统，他在 1933 年 3 月 4 日发表了这篇就职演说，简要概括了他的为政设想，并呼吁人们行动起来面对危机和重拾信心。

美文欣赏

　　This is a day of national consecration. And I am certain that my fellow Americans expect that on my induction① into the Presidency I will address them with a candor and a decision which the present situation of our Nation impels. This is preeminently② the time to speak the truth, the whole truth, frankly and boldly③. Nor need we shrink from honestly facing conditions in our country today. This great Nation will endure as it has endured④, will revive and will prosper. So, first of all, let me assert my firm belief that the only thing we have to fear is fear itself—nameless, unreasoning, unjustified terror which paralyzes⑤ needed efforts to convert retreat into advance. In every dark hour of our national life a leadership of frankness and vigor has met with that understanding and support of the people themselves which is essential to victory. I am convinced that you will again give that support to leadership in these critical days.

In such a spirit on my part and on yours we face our common difficulties. They concern, thank God, only material things. Values have shrunken⑥ to fantastic levels; taxes have risen; our ability to pay has fallen; government of all kinds is faced by serious curtailment⑦ of income; the means of exchange are frozen in the currents of trade; the withered⑧ leaves of industrial enterprise lie on every side; farmers find no markets for their produce; the savings of many years in thousands of families are gone.

More important, a host of unemployed citizens face the grim problem of existence, and an equally great number toil with little return. Only a foolish optimist can deny the dark realities of the moment.

Yet our distress comes from no failure of substance. We are stricken by no plague of locusts. Compared with the perils which our forefathers conquered because they believed and were not afraid, we have still much to be thankful for. Nature still offers her bounty and human efforts have multiplied it. Plenty is at our doorstep, but a generous use of it languishes in the very sight of the supply. Primarily this is because the rulers of the exchange of mankind's goods have failed, through their own stubbornness and their own incompetence, have admitted their failure, and have abdicated. Practices of the unscrupulous money changers stand indicted in the court of public opinion, rejected by the hearts and minds of men.

True they have tried, but their efforts have been cast in the pattern of an outworn tradition. Faced by failure of credit they have proposed only the lending of more money. Stripped of the lure of profit by which to induce our people to follow their false leadership, they have resorted to exhortations, pleading tearfully for restored confidence. They know only the rules of a generation of self-seekers. They have no vision, and when there is no vision the people perish⑨.

The money changers have fled from their high seats in the temple of our civilization. We may now restore that temple to the ancient truths. The measure of the restoration lies in the extent to which we apply social values more noble than mere monetary profit.

Happiness lies not in the mere possession of money; it lies in the joy of achievement, in the thrill of creative effort. The joy and moral stimulation of work no longer must be forgotten in the mad chase of evanescent profits. These dark days will be worth all they cost us if they teach us that our true destiny is not to be ministered unto but to minister to ourselves and to our fellow men.

Recognition of the falsity of material wealth as the standard of success goes hand in hand with the abandonment of the false belief that public office and high political position are to be valued only by the standards of pride of place and personal profit; and there must be an end to a conduct in banking and in business which too often has given to a sacred trust the likeness of callous and selfish wrongdoing. Small wonder that confidence languishes, for it thrives only on honesty, on honor, on the sacredness of obligations, on faithful protection, on unselfish performance; without them it cannot live.

Restoration calls, however, not for changes in ethics alone. This Nation asks for action, and action now.

Our greatest primary task is to put people to work. This is no unsolvable problem if we face it wisely and courageously. It can be accomplished in part by direct recruiting by the Government itself, treating the task as we would treat the emergency of a war, but at the same time, through this employment, accomplishing greatly needed projects to stimulate and reorganize the use of our natural resources.

Hand in hand with this we must frankly recognize the overbalance of population in our industrial centers and, by engaging on a national scale in a redistribution, endeavor to provide a better use of the land for those best fitted for the land. The task can be helped by definite efforts to raise the values of agricultural products and with this the power to purchase the output of our cities. It can be helped by preventing realistically the tragedy of the growing loss through foreclosure of our small homes and our farms. It can be helped by insistence that the Federal, State, and local governments act forthwith on the demand that their cost be drastically reduced. It can be helped by the unifying of relief activities which today are often scattered, uneconomical, and unequal. It can be helped by national planning for and supervision of all forms of transportation and of communications and other utilities which have a definitely public character. There are many ways in which it can be helped, but it can never be helped merely by talking about it. We must act and act quickly.

Finally, in our progress toward a resumption⑩ of work, we require two safeguards against a return of the evils of the old order; there must be a strict supervision of all banking and credits and investments; there must be an end to speculation with other people's money, and there must be provision for an adequate but sound currency.

These, my friends, are the lines of attack. I shall presently urge upon a new Congress in special session detailed measures for their fulfillment, and I shall seek the immediate assistance of the several States.

Through this program of action we address ourselves to putting our own national house in order and making income balance outgo. Our international trade relations, though vastly important, are in point of time and necessity secondary to the establishment of a sound national economy. I favor as a practical policy the putting of first things first. I shall spare no effort to restore world trade by international economic readjustment, but the emergency at home cannot wait on that accomplishment.

The basic thought that guides these specific means of national recovery is not narrowly nationalistic. It is the insistence, as a first consideration, upon the interdependence of the various elements in all parts of the United States—a recognition of the old and permanently important manifestation of the American spirit of the pioneer. It is the way to recovery. It is the immediate way. It is the strongest assurance that the recovery will endure.

In the field of world policy I would dedicate this Nation to the policy of the good neighbor—the neighbor who resolutely respects himself and, because he does so, respects the rights of others—the neighbor who respects his obligations and respects the sanctity⑪ of his agreements in and with a world of neighbors.

If I read the temper of our people correctly, we now realize, as we have never realized before, our interdependence on each other; that we can not merely take, but we must give as well; that if we are to go forward, we must move as a trained and loyal army willing to sacrifice for the good of a common discipline, because without such discipline no progress can be made, no leadership becomes effective. We are, I know, ready and willing to submit our lives and property to such discipline, because it makes possible a leadership which aims at a larger good. This I propose to offer, pledging that the larger purposes will bind upon us all as a sacred obligation with a unity of duty hitherto[12] evoked only in times of armed strife.

With this pledge taken, I assume unhesitatingly the leadership of this great army of our people dedicated to a disciplined attack upon our common problems.

Action in this image and to this end is feasible under the form of government which we have inherited from our ancestors. Our Constitution is so simple and practical that it is possible always to meet extraordinary needs by changes in emphasis and arrangement without loss of essential form. That is why our constitutional[13] system has proved itself the most superbly enduring political mechanism the modern world has produced. It has met every stress of vast expansion[14] of territory, of foreign wars, of bitter internal strife[15], of world relations.

It is to be hoped that the normal balance of executive and legislative[16] authority may be wholly adequate to meet the unprecedented[17] task before us. But it may be that an unprecedented demand and need for undelayed action may call for temporary departure from that normal balance of public procedure.

I am prepared under my constitutional duty to recommend the measures that a stricken nation in the midst of a stricken world may require. These measures, or such other measures as the Congress may build out of its experience and wisdom, I shall seek, within my constitutional authority, to bring to speedy adoption.

But in the event that the Congress shall fail to take one of these two courses, and in the event that the national emergency is still critical, I shall not evade the clear course of duty that will then confront me. I shall ask the Congress for the one remaining instrument to meet the crisis—broad executive power to wage a war against the emergency, as great as the power that would be given to me if we were in fact invaded by a foreign foe.

For the trust reposed[18] in me, I will return the courage and the devotion that befit the time. I can do no less.

We face the arduous days that lie before us in the warm courage of the national unity; with the clear consciousness of seeking old and precious moral values; with the clean satisfaction that comes from the stern performance of duty by old and young alike. We aim at the assurance of a rounded and permanent national life.

We do not distrust the future of essential democracy[19]. The people of the United

States have not failed. In their need they have registered a mandate that they want direct, vigorous[20] action. They have asked for discipline and direction under leadership. They have made me the present instrument of their wishes. In the spirit of the gift I take it.

In this dedication of a Nation we humbly ask the blessing of God. May He protect each and every one of us. May He guide me in the days to come.

词汇释义

① **induction** [ɪnˈdʌkʃn] n. 就职，就职典礼
② **preeminently** [ˌpriːˈemɪnəntli] adv. 卓越地，杰出地
③ **boldly** [ˈbəʊldli] adv. 大胆地；显眼地；冒失地
④ **endure** [ɪnˈdjʊə(r)] v. 忍受；持续
⑤ **paralyze** [ˈpærəlaɪz] v. 瘫痪，麻痹
⑥ **shrink** [ʃrɪŋk] v. 收缩；畏缩
⑦ **curtailment** [kɜːˈteɪlmənt] n. 缩减，缩短
⑧ **withered** [ˈwɪðəd] adj. 枯萎的，凋谢的，憔悴的
⑨ **perish** [ˈperɪʃ] v. 死亡，丧生，毁灭；腐烂，枯萎；老化
⑩ **resumption** [rɪˈzʌmpʃn] n. 重新开始，继续
⑪ **sanctity** [ˈsæŋktəti] n. 圣洁，神圣；不可侵犯
⑫ **hitherto** [ˌhɪðəˈtuː] adv. 到目前为止；迄今；至今
⑬ **constitutional** [ˌkɒnstɪˈtjuːʃnl] adj. 宪法的，章程的
⑭ **expansion** [ɪkˈspænʃn] n. 扩大；扩张
⑮ **strife** [straɪf] n. 斗争；争吵；冲突
⑯ **legislative** [ˈledʒɪslətɪv] adj. 立法的；立法决定的
⑰ **unprecedented** [ʌnˈpresɪdentɪd] adj. 前所未有的，史无前例的
⑱ **repose** [rɪˈpəʊz] v. 将（手臂等）靠在某人（某物）上
⑲ **democracy** [dɪˈmɒkrəsi] n. 民主（制度）；民主国家
⑳ **vigorous** [ˈvɪɡərəs] adj. 有力的；精力充沛的；充满活力的

难句解析

1. In every dark hour of our national life a leadership of frankness and vigor has

met with that understanding and support of the people themselves which is essential to victory.

【译文】 凡在我国生活阴云密布的时刻,坦率而有活力的领导都得到过人民的理解和支持,从而为胜利准备了必不可少的条件。

【解析】 "meet with" 译为 "会晤";"is essential to" 译为 "对……有必要"。

2. Stripped of the lure of profit by which to induce our people to follow their false leadership, they have resorted to exhortations, pleading tearfully for restored confidence.

【译文】 没有了当诱饵引诱人民追随他们的错误领导的金钱,他们只得求助于讲道,含泪祈求人民重新给予他们信心。

【解析】 "stripped of" 在此处译为 "脱离,离开";"exhortation" 在此处译为 "敦促;极力推荐";"plead" 在此处译为 "祈求";本句中的 "stripped of" 作状语,主语为 "they"。

3. These dark days will be worth all they cost us if they teach us that our true destiny is not to be ministered unto but to minister to ourselves and to our fellow men.

【译文】 如果这些暗淡的时日能使我们认识到,我们真正的天命不是要别人侍奉,而是为自己和同胞们服务,那么,我们付出的代价就完全是值得的。

【解析】 "worth" 在此处译为 "值得","be worth all they cost us" 此处在 "all" 之后省略了关系代词 "that",是一个定语从句;"not... but..." 译为 "不是……而是……";"to be ministered" 和 "to minister" 分别使用被动和主动的形式将 "我们" 的使命详细描述出来。

4. It is to be hoped that the normal balance of executive and legislative authority may be wholly adequate to meet the unprecedented task before us.

【译文】 而我们还希望行使法律的人士做到充分的平等,能充分地担负前所未有的任务。

【解析】 "It is to be hoped that …" 是句型 "It is hoped that …" 的变体,表达 "希望" 的意思;"be wholly adequate to" 在此处译为 "充分地";"meet" 在此处译为 "担负"。

5. But in the event that the Congress shall fail to take one of these two courses, and in the event that the national emergency is still critical, I shall not evade the clear course of duty that will then confront me.

[译文] 但是，如果国会未能采取这两种做法中的一种，并且如果国家紧急状态仍然很严重，我将不会逃避我将面临的明确职责。

[解析] "event"之后的"that"引导同位语从句，对"event"一词的内容进行解释说明。

参考译文

罗斯福总统就职演说

今天，对我们的国家来说，是一个神圣的日子。我肯定，同胞们都期待我在就任总统时，会像我国目前形势所要求的那样，坦率而果断地向他们讲话。现在正是坦白、勇敢地说出实话，说出全部实话的最好时刻。我们不必畏首畏尾，要老老实实面对我国今天的情况。这个伟大的国家会一如既往地坚持下去，它会复兴和繁荣起来。因此，让我首先表明我的坚定信念：我们唯一不得不害怕的就是害怕本身——一种莫名其妙、丧失理智、毫无根据的恐惧，它把人所需的种种努力化为泡影。凡在我国生活阴云密布的时刻，坦率而有活力的领导都得到过人民的理解和支持，从而为胜利准备了必不可少的条件。我相信，在目前危急时刻，大家会再次给予同样的支持。

我和你们都要以这种精神，来面对我们共同的困难。感谢上帝，这些困难只是物质方面的。价值被难以想象地贬缩了；课税增加了；我们的支付能力下降了；各级政府面临着严重的收入短缺；交易方式在贸易过程中遭到了冻结；工业企业枯萎的落叶到处可见；农场主的产品找不到销路；千家万户多年的积蓄付之东流。

更重要的是，大批失业公民正面临严峻的生存问题，还有大批公民正以艰辛的劳动换取微薄的报酬。只有愚蠢的乐天派会否认当前这些阴暗的现实。

但是，我们的苦恼绝不是因为缺乏物资。我们没有遭到什么蝗虫灾害。我们的先辈曾以信念和无畏一次次转危为安，比起他们经历过的险阻，我们仍大可感到欣慰。大自然仍在给予我们恩惠，人类的努力已使之倍增。富足的情景近在咫尺，但就在我们见到这种情景的时候，宽裕的生活却悄然离去。这主要是因为主宰人类物资交换的统治者们失败了，他们固执己见而又无能为力，因而已经认定失败了，并撒手不管了。贪得无厌的货币兑换商的种种行径，将受到舆论法庭的起诉，将受到人类心灵理智的唾弃。

是的，他们是努力过，然而他们用的是一种完全过时的方法。面对信贷的失败，他们只是提议借出更多的钱。没有了当诱饵引诱人民追随他们的错误领导的金钱，他们只得求助于井道，含泪祈求人民重新给予他们信心。他们只知自我追求者们的处世规则。他们没有眼光，而没有眼光的人是要灭亡的。

如今，货币兑换商已从我们文明庙宇的高处落荒而逃。我们要以千古不变的真理来重建这座庙宇。衡量这重建的尺度是我们体现比金钱利益更高尚的社会价值的程度。

幸福并不在于单纯地占有金钱；幸福还在于取得成就后的喜悦，在于创造性努力时的激情。务必不能再忘记劳动带来的喜悦和激励，而去疯狂地追逐那转瞬即逝的利润。如果这些暗淡的时日能使我们认识到，我们真正的天命不是要别人侍奉，而是为自己和同胞们服务，那么，我们付出的代价就完全是值得的。

认识到把物质财富当作成功的标准是错误的，我们就会抛弃以地位尊严和个人收益为唯一标准，来衡量公职和高级政治地位的错误信念；我们必须制止银行界和企业界的一种行为，这种行为常常使神圣的委托混同于无情和自私的不正当行为。难怪信心在减弱，信心，只能靠诚实、信誉、忠心维护和无私履行职责。而没有这些，就不可能有信心。

但是，复兴不仅仅只要改变伦理观念。这个国家要求行动起来，现在就行动起来。

我们最大、最基本的任务是让人民投入工作。只要我们行之以智慧和勇气，这个问题就可以解决。这可以部分由政府本身直接征募完成，就像对待临战的紧要关头一样，但同时，在有了人手的情况下，我们还急需能刺激并重组巨大自然资源的工程。

我们齐心协力，但必须坦白地承认工业中心的人口失衡，我们必须在全国范围内重新分配，使土地在最适合的人手中发挥更大作用。明确地为提高农产品价值并以此购买城市产品所做的努力，会有助于任务的完成。避免许多小家庭业、农场业被取消赎取抵押品的权利的悲剧也有助于任务的完成。联邦、州、各地政府立即行动回应要求降价的呼声，有助于任务的完成。将现在常常是分散、不经济、不平等的救济活动统一起来有助于任务的完成。

对所有公共交通运输，通信及其他涉及公众生活的设施作全国性的计划及监督有助于任务的完成。许多事情都有助于任务完成，但这些绝不包括空谈。我们必须行动，立即行动。

最后，为了重新开始工作，我们需要两手防御，来抗御旧秩序恶魔卷土重来；一定要有严格监督银行业、信贷及投资的机制；一定要杜绝投机；一定要有充足而健康的货币供应。

以上这些，朋友们，就是施政方针。我要在特别会议上敦促新国会给予详细实施方案，并且，我要向一些州请求立即的援助。

通过行动，我们将予以我们自己一个有秩序的国家大厦，使收入大于支出。我们的国际贸易，虽然很重要，但现在在时间和必要性上，次于对本国健康经济的建立。我建议，作为可行的策略，首要事务先行。虽然我将不遗余力通过国际经济重新协调来恢复国际贸易，但我认为国内的紧急情况无法等待这重新协调的完成。

指导这一特别的全国性复苏的基本思想并非狭隘的国家主义。我首先考虑的是坚持美国这一整体中各部分的相互依赖性——这是对美国式的开拓精神的古老而永恒证明的体现。这才是复苏之路，是即时之路，是保证复苏功效持久之路。

在国际政策方面，我将使美国采取睦邻友好的政策。做一个决心自重，因此而尊重邻国的国家。做一个履行义务，尊重与他国协约的国家。

如果我对人民的心情的了解正确的话，我想我们已认识到了我们从未认识的问题，我们是互相依存的，我们不可以只索取，我们还必须奉献。我们前进时，必须像一支训练有素的忠诚的军队，愿意为共同的原则而献身，因为，没有这些原则，就无法取得进步，领导就不可能得力。我们都已做好准备，并愿意为此原则献出生命和财产，因为这将使志在建设更美好社会的领导成为可能。我倡议，为了更伟大的目标，我们所有的人，以一致的职责紧紧团结起来。这是神圣的义务，非战乱，不停止。

有了这样的誓言，我将毫不犹豫地承担领导伟大人民大军的任务，致力于对我们普遍问题的强攻。

这样的行动，这样的目标，在我们从祖先手中接过的政府中是可行的。我们的宪法如此简单、实用。它随时可以应对特殊情况，只需对重点和安排加以修改而不丧失中心思想，正因为如此，我们的宪法体制已自证为是最有适应性的政治体制。它已应对过巨大的国土扩张、外战、内乱及国际关系所带来的压力。

而我们还希望行使法律的人士做到充分的平等，能充分地担负前所未有的任务。但现在前所未有的对紧急行动的需要要求国民暂时丢弃平常生活节奏，紧迫起来。

根据我的宪法义务，我准备好建议一个在受灾世界中受灾的国家可能需要的措施。这些措施，或国会根据其经验和智慧可能建立的其他措施，我将在我的宪法权力范围内寻求尽快通过。

但是，如果国会未能采取这两种做法中的一种，并且如果国家紧急状态仍然很严重，我将不会逃避我将面临的明确职责。我将要求国会提供应对危机的剩余工具——广泛的行政权力，以对抗紧急情况，如果我们实际上被外国敌人入侵，我将获得的权力一样大。

对于寄托在我身上的信任，我将回报与时间相称的勇气和奉献。我决不食言。

让我们正视面前的严峻岁月，怀着举国一致给我们带来的热情和勇气，怀着寻求传统的、珍贵的道德观念的明确意识，怀着老老少少都能通过恪尽职守而得到的问心无愧的满足。我们的目标是要保证国民生活的圆满和长治久安。

我们并不怀疑基本民主制度的未来。合众国人民并没有失败。他们在困难中表达了自己的委托，即要求采取直接而有力的行动。他们要求有领导的纪律和方向。他们现在选择了我作为实现他们的愿望的工具。我接受这份厚赠。

在此举国奉献之际，我们谦卑地请求上帝赐福。愿上帝保佑我们大家每一个人，愿上帝在未来的日子里指引我。

读后写作

Franklin D. Roosevelt is one of the greatest presidents in the history of the USA. Can you say something about him and his achievement?

Blood, Toil, Tears and Sweat
带着血泪和汗水抗争到底
—— Winston Churchill

读前导语

本篇文章作者温斯顿·丘吉尔（1874—1965），英国政治家、历史学家、演说家、作家、记者，第61、63届英国首相。

丘吉尔出任首相于危难之际，面临的压力和困难可想而知，他迫切希望得到公众的信任和支持。他以真挚的情感向大家吐露自己的肺腑之言。他说："我没有什么可以奉献，除了鲜血、勤劳、汗水与眼泪。我们正面临一场十分严峻的考验。我们将经历数月的战斗与磨难。"

这篇演讲言辞坚定，明确有力，掷地有声，充满着必胜的决心和信心。在演讲中，他以自问自答的形式斩钉截铁地告诉听众，目前的政策就是要与敌人决一死战；目的就是胜利，一定要夺取胜利！最后，他号召大家："来吧，让我们团结一致，并肩前进。"这就使得这篇演讲犹如进军号角，振奋人心，极大地鼓舞了国民与法西斯血战到底的斗志。

美文欣赏

On Friday evening last I received from His Majesty the mission to form a new administration. It was the evident[①] will of Parliament and the nation that this should be conceived[②] on the broadest possible basis and that it should include all parties. I have already completed the most important part of this task. A war cabinet has been formed of five members, representing, with the Labor, Opposition and Liberals, the unity of the nation. It was necessary that this should be done in one single day on account of the extreme urgency and rigor③ of events. Other key positions were filled yesterday. I am submitting④ a further list to the King tonight. I hope to complete the appointment of principal Ministers during tomorrow. The appointment of other Ministers usually takes a little longer. I trust when Parliament meets again this part of my task will be completed and that the administration will be complete in all respects.

I considered it in the public interest to suggest to the Speaker that the House should be summoned today. At the end of today's proceedings⑤, the adjournment⑥ of the House will be proposed until May 21st with provision for earlier meeting if need be. Business for that will be notified to M. P.'s at the earliest opportunity. I now invite the House by a resolution to record its approval of the steps taken and declare its confidence in the new government. The resolution:

"That this House welcomes the formation⑦ of a government representing the united and inflexible resolve⑧ of the nation to prosecute⑨ the war with Germany to a victorious conclusion."

To form an administration of this scale and complexity⑩ is a serious undertaking in itself. But we are in the preliminary phase of one of the greatest battles in history. We are in action at many other points—in Norway and in Holland—and we have to be prepared in the Mediterranean. The air battle is continuing, and many preparations have to be made here at home. In this crisis I think I may be pardoned if I do not address the House at any length today, and I hope that any of my friends and colleagues or former colleagues who are affected by the political reconstruction will make all allowances⑪ for any lack of ceremony with which it has been necessary to act. I say to the House as I said to Ministers who have joined this government, I have nothing to offer but blood, toil, tears, and sweat. We have before us an ordeal of the most grievous⑫ kind. We have before us many, many months of struggle and suffering.

You ask, what is our policy? I say it is to wage war by land, sea, and air. War with all our might and with all the strength God has given us, and to wage war against a monstrous tyranny never surpassed⑬ in the dark and lamentable⑭ catalogue of human crime. That is our policy. You ask, what is our aim? I can answer in one word. It is victory. Victory at all costs—victory in spite of all terrors—victory, however long and hard the road may be, for without victory there is no survival. Let that be realized. No survival for the British Empire, no survival for all that the British Empire has stood for, no survival for the urge, the impulse⑮ of the ages, that mankind shall move forward toward his goal. But I take up my task in buoyancy⑯ and hope. I feel sure that our cause will not be suffered to fail among men. I feel entitled at this juncture⑰, at this time, to claim the aid of all and to say, "Come then, let us go forward together with our united strength."

词汇释义

①**evident** ['evɪdənt] *adj.* 清楚的；显然的

②**conceive** [kən'siːv] *v.* 想象，构想；认为

③**rigor** ['rɪgə(r)] *n.* 严格；严酷；严密

④**submit** [səb'mɪt] *v.* 呈递，提交；屈服

⑤**proceeding** [prə'siːdɪŋ] *n.* 诉讼；进行，进程；行动

⑥**adjournment** [ə'dʒɜːnmənt] *n.* 休会；延期；休会期；休庭期

⑦**formation** [fɔː'meɪʃn] *n.* 形成；构成；结构

⑧**resolve** [rɪ'zɒlv] *n.* 决议，决定，坚决

⑨**prosecute** ['prɒsɪkjuːt] *v.* 控告，起诉；继续从事

⑩**complexity** [kəm'pleksəti] *n.* 诉讼；复杂性

⑪**allowance** [ə'laʊəns] *n.* 津贴；补助

⑫**grievous** ['griːvəs] *adj.* 令人伤心或痛苦的；(指坏事) 剧烈的

⑬**surpass** [sə'pɑːs] *vt.* 超过；优于；胜过；非……所能办到

⑭**lamentable** [lə'mentəbl] *adj.* 可悲的，令人惋惜的

⑮**impulse** ['ɪmpʌls] *n.* 凭冲动行事；突如其来的念头

⑯**buoyancy** ['bɔɪənsi] *n.* 浮力；(物体在液体里的) 浮性

⑰**juncture** ['dʒʌŋktʃə(r)] *n.* 时刻，关键时刻；接合点

难句解析

1. It was the evident will of Parliament and the nation that this should be conceived on the broadest possible basis and that it should include all parties.

译文 很显然，议会和国家都希望新政府的组成范围尽可能宽广，能够包

含所有政党。

[解析] "It was the evident will of Parliament and the nation that …"是一个主语从句，其中"will"一词译为"希望，意愿"。

2. I trust when Parliament meets again this part of my task will be completed and that the administration will be complete in all respects.

[译文] 不过我相信，我能在下次议会召开之前完成这项工作，届时政府各部门都会处于完善状态。

[解析] "I trust when … and that …"中的"trust"引导宾语从句；"in all aspects"译为"在各方面"。

3. In this crisis I think I may be pardoned if I do not address the House at any length today, and I hope that any of my friends and colleagues or former colleagues who are affected by the political reconstruction will make all allowances for any lack of ceremony with which it has been necessary to act.

[译文] 因为国家正处于危机中，我觉得，如果我今天选择不在下议院发表就职演讲也情有可原，我希望我的所有朋友、同事，以及因为这次政府重组而成为前同事的人，都能体谅我放弃这些不必要的礼仪行为。

[解析] "I think I may be pardoned if…"中的"I think"引导宾语从句，"if"引导条件状语从句；"I hope that any of my friends and colleagues or former colleagues who are affected by the political reconstruction will make all allowances for any lack of ceremony with which it has been necessary to act."中的"that"引导宾语从句，"who"引导定语从句，修饰先行词"any of my friends and colleagues or former colleagues"，在定语从句中充当主语。

4. No survival for the British Empire, no survival for all that the British Empire has stood for, no survival for the urge, the impulse of the ages, that mankind shall move forward toward his goal.

[译文] 如果我们战败，大英帝国就将不复存在，大英帝国所代表、所捍卫的一切也将不复存在，推动时代前进、人类进步的动力也将不复存在。

[解析] 本句中排比句式的使用比较令人震撼，表明"我们"所处的关键历史时刻，"带着血泪和汗水抗争到底"刻不容缓。

参考译文

带着血泪和汗水抗争到底

上周五晚上，我受国王陛下委托，奉命组建新政府。很显然，议会和国家都希望新政府的组成范围尽可能宽广，能够包含所有政党。我已完成最关键的组建工作。战时内阁已经成立，包含部分来自工党、反对党和自由党的5名成员，以展现我国团结一致。鉴于当前事态艰难紧迫，我必须在一天内完成组建内阁的工作。昨天，我已完成任命其他重要岗位的官员。今晚，我会向国王递交一份任命名单。明天，我打算完成任命各部门大臣的工作。完成任命其他部门大臣的工作，应该需要更多时间。不过我相信，我能在下次议会召开之前完成这项工作，届时政府各部门都会处于完善状态。

我认为，议长在今天召集下议院是符合公众利益的。今天的会议结束后，如果不出意外的话，下议院会休会到5月21日。如休会期间需提前召开会议，我们会尽早通知各位议员。我请求下议院通过一份决议，以示对我们政策的支持和对新政府的信任。决议如下：

"下议院同意组建新政府，代表国家团结一致、坚定不移与德国继续战争，并取得最后胜利的决心。"

组建这么一个庞大又复杂的管理机构本身就是一项严峻任务。不过我们正处于史上一场最伟大战役的初期。我们在许多地区作战——挪威与荷兰——我们还要时刻准备在地中海进行作战。空战从未停止，我们在本土也要做好备战工作。因为国家正处于危机中，我觉得，如果我今天选择不在下议院发表就职演讲也情有可原，我希望我的所有朋友、同事，以及因为这次政府重组而成为前同事的人，都能体谅我放弃这些不必要的礼仪行为。我想对下议院和本政府的各大臣说，我没有什么可以奉献，除了鲜血、勤劳、汗水与眼泪。我们正面临一场十分严峻的考验。我们将经历数月的战斗与磨难。

你问，我们的政策是什么？我可以回答你，那就是在海陆空继续作战。使用我们自己的，和上帝赐予我们的一切力量继续作战，继续对抗这个人类历史上前所未有的恐怖暴政。这就是我们的政策。你问，我们的目标是什么？我可以用一个词回答。那就是胜利。不惜一切代价取得胜利，不惧一切敌人取得胜利。无论前方的道路多么黑暗漫长,也要取得胜利,因为不取得胜利,我们就会面临灭顶之灾。所有人都要认识到这一点。如果我们战败,大英帝国就将不复存在,大英帝国所代表、所捍卫的一切也将不复存在,推动时代前进、人类进步的动力也将不复存在。我抱有乐观的态度,满怀希望地接受任务。我坚信我们的事业不会失败。我觉得在此关键时刻,我有资格对所有人说:"来吧,让我们团结一致,并肩前进。"

读后写作

When Churchill delivered the famous speech, he was quite confident that his country will be the winner of the war, which inspired his people a lot. Please try to give a speech to make your friend be confident to pass some important exams.

Arm Yourselves and Be Ye Men of Valour
鼓起勇气
—— Winston Churchill

读前导语

本篇文章作者温斯顿·丘吉尔（1874—1965），英国政治家、历史学家、演说家、作家、记者，第61、63届英国首相。

1940年5月19日，英国首相丘吉尔首次发表全国讲话，为英国人民讲述战争形势，他承认德军击穿了盟军防线，在盟军后方穿插，致使盟军陷入险境，同时他也鼓舞英国人民不要丧失勇气和信心，盟军一定会取得胜利。

美文欣赏

I speak to you for the first time as Prime Minister in a solemn[①] hour for the life of our country, of our empire, of our allies, and, above all, of the cause of freedom. A tremendous[②] battle is raging in France and Flanders. The Germans, by a remarkable combination of air bombing and heavily armored tanks, have broken through the French defenses north of the Maginot Line, and strong columns of their armored vehicles are ravaging[③] the open country, which for the first day or two was without defenders. They have penetrated deeply and spread alarm and confusion in their track. Behind them there are now appearing infantry in lorries, and behind them, again, the large masses are moving forward. The re-groupment of the French armies to make head against, and also to strike at, this intruding wedge has been proceeding for several days, largely assisted by the magnificent efforts of the Royal Air Force.

We must not allow ourselves to be intimidated by the presence of these armored vehicles in unexpected places behind our lines. If they are behind our Front, the French are also at many points fighting actively behind theirs. Both sides are therefore in an extremely dangerous position. And if the French Army and our own Army are well handled, as I believe they will be, if the French retain that genius for recovery and counter-attack for which they have so long been famous, and if the British Army shows the dogged endurance and solid fighting power of which there have been so many examples in the past, then a sudden transformation of the scene might spring into being.

Now it would be foolish, however, to disguise the gravity of the hour. It would be still more foolish to lose heart and courage or to suppose that well-trained, well-equipped armies numbering three or four millions of men can be overcome in the space of a few weeks, or even months, by a scoop, or raid of mechanized vehicles, however formidable[4]. We may look with confidence to the stabilization[5] of the Front in France, and to the general engagement of the masses, which will enable the qualities of the French and British soldiers to be matched squarely against those of their adversaries. For myself, I have invincible confidence in the French Army and its leaders. Only a very small part of that splendid Army has yet been heavily engaged; and only a very small part of France has yet been invaded. There is a good evidence to show that practically the whole of the specialized and mechanized forces of the enemy have been already thrown into the battle; and we know that very heavy losses have been inflicted[6] upon them. No officer or man, no brigade or division, which grapples at close quarters with the enemy, wherever encountered, can fail to make a worthy contribution to the general result. The Armies must cast away the idea of resisting attack behind concrete lines or natural obstacles, and must realize that mastery can only be regained by furious and unrelenting assault. And this spirit must not only animate the High Command, but must inspire every fighting man.

In the air—often at serious odds, often at odds hitherto thought overwhelming—we have been clawing down three or four to one of our enemies; and the relative balance of the British and German Air Forces is now considerably more favorable to us than at the beginning of the battle. In cutting down the German bombers, we are fighting our own battle as well as that of France. My confidence in our ability to fight it out to the finish with the German Air Force has been strengthened by the fierce encounters⑦ which have taken place and are taking place. At the same time, our heavy bombers are striking nightly at the tap-root of German mechanized power, and have already inflicted serious damage upon the oil refineries on which the Nazi effort to dominate the world directly depends.

We must expect that as soon as stability is reached on the Western Front, the bulk⑧ of that hideous apparatus of aggression which gashed Holland into ruin and slavery in a few days will be turned upon us. I am sure I speak for all when I say we are ready to face it, to endure it, and to retaliate against it to any extent that the unwritten laws of war permit. There will be many men and many women in this Island who, when the ordeal comes upon them, as come it will, will feel comfort, and even a pride, that they are sharing the perils of our lads at the Front—soldiers, sailors, and airmen—God bless them—and are drawing away from them a part at least of the onslaught⑨ they have to bear. Is not this the appointed time for all to make the utmost exertions in their power? If the battle is to be won, we must provide our men with ever-increasing quantities of the weapons and ammunition⑩ they need. We must have, and have quickly, more aeroplanes, more tanks, more shells, more guns. There is imperious need for these vital munitions. They increase our strength against the powerfully armed enemy. They replace the wastage⑪ of the obstinate struggle—and the knowledge that wastage will speedily be replaced enables us to draw more readily upon our reserves and throw them in now that everything counts so much.

Our task is not only to win the battle—but to win the war. After this battle in France abates its force, there will come the battle for our Island—for all Britain is, and all that Britain means. That will be the struggle. In that supreme emergency we shall not hesitate to take every step, even the most drastic, to call forth from our people the last ounce and the last inch of effort of which they are capable. The interests of property, the hours of labor, are nothing compared to the struggle for life and honor, for right and freedom, to which we have vowed ourselves.

I have received from the Chiefs of the French Republic, and in particular from its indomitable⑫ Prime Minister, Monsieur Reynaud, the most sacred pledges⑬ that whatever happens they will fight to the end, be it bitter or be it glorious. Nay, if we fight to the end, it can only be glorious.

Having received His Majesty's commission, I have formed an Administration of men and women of every Party and of almost every point of view. We have differed and quarrelled in the past, but now one bond unites us all: to wage war until victory is won, and never to surrender⑭ ourselves to servitude and shame, whatever the cost and the agony may be. This is one of the most awe-striking periods in the long history of France and Britain. It is also beyond doubt the most sublime⑮. Side by side, unaided⑯ except by their kith and kin in the great Dominions and by the wide empires which rest beneath their shield—side by side the British and French peoples have advanced to rescue not only Europe but mankind from the foulest⑰ and most soul-destroying tyranny which has ever darkened and stained the pages of history. Behind them, behind us, behind the Armies and Fleets of Britain and France, gather a group of shattered States and bludgeoned⑱ races: the Czechs, the Poles, the Norwegians, the Danes, the Dutch, the Belgians—upon all of whom the long night of barbarism will descend, unbroken even by a star of hope, unless we conquer, as conquer we must, as conquer we shall.

Today is Trinity Sunday. Centuries ago words were written to be a call and a spur⑲ to the faithful servants of truth and justice:

Arm yourselves, and be ye men of valour, and be in readiness for the conflict; for it is better for us to perish in battle than to look upon the outrage⑳ of our nation and our altars. As the will of God is in Heaven, even so let it be.

词汇释义

①**solemn** ['sɒləm] *adj.* 庄严的，严肃的；庄重的

②**tremendous** [trə'mendəs] *adj.* 极大的，巨大的；可怕的

③**ravage** ['rævɪdʒ] *v.* 毁坏；劫掠

④**formidable** [fə'mɪdəbl] *adj.* 可怕的；令人敬畏的

⑤**stabilization** [ˌsteɪbəlaɪ'zeɪʃn] *n.* 稳定性；稳定化；安定面

⑥**inflict** [ɪn'flɪkt] *v.* 使承受，使遭受；给予（打击等）

⑦**encounter** [ɪn'kaʊntə(r)] *v.* 遭遇；偶遇 *n.* 偶遇，邂逅

⑧**bulk** [bʌlk] *n.*（大）体积；大部分；庞大的身躯；主体

⑨**onslaught** [ˈɒnslɔːt] *n.* 猛攻，攻击；突击；大量

⑩**ammunition** [ˌæmjəˈnɪʃn] *n.* 弹药；事实

⑪**wastage** [ˈweɪstɪdʒ] *n.* 消耗；废物；浪费；消融

⑫**indomitable** [ɪnˈdɒmɪtəbl] *adj.* 不屈服的，不气馁的

⑬**pledge** [pledʒ] *n.* 保证，誓言；抵押权；公约

⑭**surrender** [səˈrendə(r)] *v.* 投降；屈服；自首

⑮**sublime** [səˈblaɪm] *adj.* 庄严的，雄伟的；令人赞叹的

⑯**unaided** [ʌnˈeɪdɪd] *adj.* 无外援的，独立的

⑰**foul** [faʊl] *adj.* 犯规的；邪恶的；难闻的，有恶臭的；下流的

⑱**bludgeon** [ˈblʌdʒən] *v.* 用棍棒打，重击

⑲**spur** [spɜː(r)] *n.* 马刺；鞭策；激励；（公路或铁路的）支线

⑳**outrage** [ˈaʊtreɪdʒ] *n.* 义愤；愤慨；暴行；骇人听闻的事件

难句解析

1. I speak to you for the first time as Prime Minister in a solemn hour for the life of our country, of our empire, of our allies, and, above all, of the cause of freedom.

[译文] 这是我第一次以首相身份对你们讲话，在这一生死攸关的时刻，我想同你们谈及我们国家、我们的大英帝国、我们的盟国，以及我们最关键的自由事业。

[解析] "for the first time" 译为"第一次，首次"；"in a solemn hour" 译为"在这庄严的时刻"；"of our country, of our empire, of our allies, and, above all, of the cause of freedom"，此处的几个 of 短语涉及的对象不断扩大、提升，引发听众强烈的共鸣，能起到团结民众进行斗争的巨大作用。

2. And if the French Army and our own Army are well handled, as I believe they will be, if the French retain that genius for recovery and counter-attack for which they have so long been famous, and if the British Army shows the dogged endurance and solid fighting power of which there have been so many examples in the past, then a sudden transformation of the scene might spring into being.

[译文] 只要法军和我军能妥善处理好当前的战况；只要法军能发挥出自己

一直以来闻名于世的重组反击特长；只要英军像过去几天那样，继续发挥出顽强的耐力和强大的战斗力，那么我们就可以顷刻间扭转战局，我相信我们可以做到。

[解析] 本句中由"if"引导的条件状语从句将当时战争能够胜利的条件分析得清晰和透彻，"as I believe they will be"是插入语，用以表达首相对于本国军队和法国军队的坚定信心；"genius"译为"天赋，特长"，此处用来描写法军在重组反击方面的巨大优势。

3. There is a good evidence to show that practically the whole of the specialized and mechanized forces of the enemy have been already thrown into the battle; and we know that very heavy losses have been inflicted upon them.

[译文] 我们有信心认为，敌军战斗力最强的机械化部队已经全部投入战斗；而且我们还知道，这支部队损失惨重。

[解析] "There is a good evidence to show that…"中的"that"引导宾语从句；"be inflicted upon"译为"遭受打击"。

4. My confidence in our ability to fight it out to the finish with the German Air Force has been strengthened by the fierce encounters which have taken place and are taking place.

[译文] 我希望已经发生的和正在发生的激烈空战，可以让我们对皇家空军的能力更有信心，相信他们能彻底战胜德国空军。

[解析] "which"引导定语从句，修饰之前的"the fierce encounters"，在从句中充当主语；"have taken place and are taking place"在说明"我"对于本次战争的坚定信心，认为"我们"必将击败德军，获得胜利。

5. Having received His Majesty's commission, I have formed an Administration of men and women of every Party and of almost every point of view.

[译文] 我受国王陛下委托，挑选了来自各个党派、持有各观点的男男女女，组建了新一届政府。

[解析] "Having received His Majesty's commission"在整个句子中作状语，表明"我"组建一个新政府的原因；"I"是整个句子的主语。

参考译文

鼓起勇气

　　这是我第一次以首相身份对你们讲话，在这一生死攸关的时刻，我想同你谈及我们国家、我们的大英帝国、我们的盟国，以及我们最关键的自由事业。法国和比利时境内爆发了激烈的战斗。德军凭借重装甲部队和空军部队的杰出配合，已突破了马奇诺防线以北的法军防线，德军强大的装甲部队正在法国开阔的国土上肆虐，在战斗开始的头一两天，他们几乎没有遭遇抵抗。德军已经深深刺穿了法军防线，一路造成巨大的恐慌与混乱。德军装甲部队突破防线后，摩托化步兵迅速跟进，大量步兵又紧跟其后。这几日，法军正在重新集结，准备在皇家空军的大力协助下，阻挡并击退敌人的锥形战术。

　　我们绝不要被这些突然出现在我军阵地后方的装甲部队吓到。如果他们攻击我军后侧，那么各地的法军也会从他们的后侧发起猛烈进攻。因此，战争形势对于敌我双方都十分危险。只要法军和我军能妥善处理好当前的战况；只要法军能发挥出自己一直以来闻名于世的重组反击特长；只要英军像过去几天那样，继续发挥出顽强的耐力和强大的战斗力，那么我们就可以顷刻间扭转战局，我相信我们可以做到。

　　如果说现在的战况无须担忧，那完全是自欺欺人。但是，如果我们觉得区区几支机械化部队发动突袭，就能在几周或几个月的时间内，击败我们三四百万训练有素、装备精良的大军，进而失去信心，丧失勇气，那才是愚不可及，无论敌人的装甲部队战斗力多么凶悍，也做不到。我们十分相信，盟军很快就能稳住法国的战线，而广大人民群众也会积极支持这场战争，届时法军士兵和英军士兵的战斗力便能与敌军不相上下。而我本人对法国军队和法军指挥官们抱有十足的信心。目前，所向披靡的法军才只出动了很小一部分军队；而法国也仅有一小部分领土被德军占领。而反观敌军，我们有信心认为，敌军战斗力最强的机械化部队已经全部投入战斗；而且我们还知道，这支部队损失惨重。无论是军官还是士兵，无论是一个旅还是一个师，无论在什么地方和敌军近距离遭遇，都要进行战斗，只要战斗，就能对整场战争做出贡献。英法联军必须摒弃依托钢筋混凝土防线，或者依托天然屏障进行防御的思想，我们必须不停地发动猛烈进攻，才能重夺战争的主动权。这种思想不仅要贯彻到最高司令部，还要贯彻到我们每一位战士的心中。

在空中——敌我差距悬殊，可以说敌人具有压倒性的优势——我方空军经常打出一比三甚至一比四的伤亡比；比起战役刚开始时，现在英德空军实力相对平衡了许多，这对我军有利。皇家空军在空中截杀德军轰炸机，这既是在帮助我们的军队，也是在帮助法军。我希望已经发生的和正在发生的激烈空战，可以让我们对皇家空军的能力更有信心，相信他们能彻底战胜德国空军。与此同时，我军的重型轰炸机每夜都在对德军机械化部队的制造厂展开空袭，对纳粹征服世界有着直接影响的炼油厂也已被我军重创。

我们必须提前预料到，一旦西线战场陷入僵持，德军曾用于摧毁并征服荷兰的可怕战争武器，就会大量转而用于攻击英国。我相信，我的这句话可以代表全体英国人民，我们已经准备好面对敌人入侵，挫败敌人入侵，并对敌人的入侵施以回击——在不成文的战争法允许的前提下，展开最猛烈的回击。当战火席卷不列颠岛时，我国的许多男男女女甚至会感到欣慰自豪，因为他们帮我们前线的小伙子们分担了危险——前线的海陆空三军，愿上帝保佑他们——他们至少帮助前线的战士们吸引了一部分火力。难道现在不是全体人民竭尽全力的时候吗？如果我们想要赢得这场战争，就必须向我们的战士提供他们日益需要的武器弹药。我们必须尽快生产更多的飞机、坦克、炮弹、火炮。现在前线急需这些重要的武器装备。这些武器可以增强我军的实力，帮助他们对抗装备精良的敌军。这些武器可以帮助我军打破僵持不下的战斗局面；待到那时，我们又需要果断利用我军的武器弹药库存，将其源源不断投入战场，这就更凸显出军工生产的重要性。

我们的任务不仅是要赢得这场战役——还要赢得这场战争。敌人在法国战役受挫后，必定会迁怒于我们的家园——届时我们要保卫整个不列颠岛，保护全体英国人民。这将是一场硬仗。在这场关乎国家存亡的紧急战斗中，我们会毫不犹豫地采取一切手段动员人民为战争倾尽全力，哪怕是极端手段也在所不惜。比起我们为生存和荣誉而发起的伟大战争，比起我们誓死要捍卫的权利与自由，失去一些财产，多一些工作时间又能算什么。

我已经从法兰西共和国的政府高层，特别是誓死不屈的法国总理雷诺先生口中得到了庄严保证，他们承诺，无论这场战争是胜利还是失败，法国都会战斗到底。不,只要我们能战斗到底,战争的结果就只有胜利。

　　我受国王陛下委托,挑选了来自各个党派、持有各观点的男男女女,组建了新一届政府。我们之间过去有过分歧和矛盾;但是现在,一条纽带将我们团结联系到了一起——我们要继续战斗,直至取得胜利,无论要付出多大的代价,无论要承受多大的痛苦,我们也不会屈膝接受耻辱奴役。现在是英法两国悠久历史上最让人敬畏的时刻之一。现在也毫无疑问是我们最为崇高的时刻。英国人民和法国人民肩并肩,在只得到两帝国治下庞大领地内人民帮助的情况下——依然正在奋勇前进,我们不仅要拯救欧洲,还要保护全人类免遭这一罪孽深重、荼毒生灵的暴政危害,德国的暴政抹黑、玷污了人类的历史篇章。在英法身后——在英国和法国海军舰队的身后——还有一支军队,这支军队的成员来自各个山河破碎的国家,来自各个饱受压迫的民族:捷克人、波兰人、挪威人、丹麦人、荷兰人、比利时人——野蛮暴政带来的漫漫长夜即将笼罩在他们头顶,即便是希望之星也无法照亮这一黑夜,唯有胜利的曙光才能粉碎它,我们必须胜利,我们也注定会胜利。

　　今天是三一主日。千百年前,有人写下这段文字,以召唤真理和正义的信徒:

　　"拿起武器,鼓起勇气,准备战斗;与其眼睁睁看着国家与祭坛惨遭践踏,不如在战斗中献出生命。既然上帝执意将其仆人召入天国,那我们就坦然进入天国吧。"

读后写作

　　The situation of the war was not favorable to the Britain, while the prime minister asked the people to be confident. Can you imagine the thought of his inner world at that time?

We Shall Fight on the Beaches（Excerpts）
我们将战斗到底（节选）
—— Winston Churchill

读前导语

本篇文章作者温斯顿·丘吉尔（1874—1965），英国政治家、历史学家、演说家、作家、记者，第61、63届英国首相。

1940年6月4日，英国首相丘吉尔在下议院发表了这篇文章以宣布英国绝不投降的态度，并鼓舞英国人民抵抗纳粹德国的入侵。

美文欣赏

The whole question of home defense against invasion is, of course, powerfully affected by the fact that we have for the time being in this Island incomparably[①] more powerful military forces than we have ever had at any moment in this war or the last. But this will not continue. We shall not be content with a defensive war. We have our duty to our Ally. We have to reconstitute and build up the British Expeditionary Force once again, under its gallant Commander-in-Chief, Lord Gort. All this is in train; but in the interval we must put our defenses in this Island into such a high state of organization that the fewest possible numbers will be required to give effective security and that the largest possible potential of offensive effort may be realized. On this we are now engaged. It will be very convenient, if it be the desire of the House, to enter upon this subject in a secret Session. Not that the government would necessarily be able to reveal in very great detail military secrets, but we like to have our discussions free, without the restraint imposed by the fact that they will be read the next day by the enemy; and the

Government would benefit by views freely expressed in all parts of the House by Members with their knowledge of so many different parts of the country. I understand that some request is to be made upon this subject, which will be readily acceded to by His Majesty's Government.

We have found it necessary to take measures of increasing stringency[②], not only against enemy aliens and suspicious[③] characters of other nationalities, but also against British subjects who may become a danger or a nuisance[④] should the war be transported to the United Kingdom. I know there are a great many people affected by the orders which we have made who are the passionate enemies of Nazi Germany. I am very sorry for them, but we cannot, at the present time and under the present stress, draw all the distinctions which we should like to do. If parachute landings were attempted and fierce fighting attendant upon them followed, these unfortunate people would be far better out of the way, for their own sakes as well as for ours. There is, however, another class, for which I feel not the slightest sympathy. Parliament has given us the powers to put down Fifth Column activities with a strong hand, and we shall use those powers subject to the supervision and correction of the House, without the slightest hesitation until we are satisfied, and more than satisfied, that this malignancy in our midst has been effectively stamped out.

Turning once again, and this time more generally, to the question of invasion, I would observe that there has never been a period in all these long centuries of which we boast when an absolute guarantee against invasion, still less against serious raids, could have been given to our people. In the days of Napoleon the same wind which would have carried his transports across the Channel might have driven away the blockading fleet. There was always the chance, and it is that chance which has excited and befooled[⑤] the imaginations of many Continental tyrants. Many are the tales that are told. We are assured that novel methods will be adopted, and when we see the originality of malice[⑥], the ingenuity[⑦] of aggression, which our enemy displays, we may certainly prepare ourselves for every kind of novel stratagem[⑧] and every kind of brutal and treacherous maneuver. I think that no idea is so outlandish[⑨] that it should not be considered and viewed with a searching, but at the same time, I hope, with a steady eye. We must never forget the solid assurances of sea power and those which belong to air power if it can be locally exercised.

　　I have, myself, full confidence that if all do their duty, if nothing is neglected⑩, and if the best arrangements are made, as they are being made, we shall prove ourselves once again able to defend our Island home, to ride out the storm of war, and to outlive the menace of tyranny, if necessary for years, if necessary alone. At any rate, that is what we are going to try to do. That is the resolve of His Majesty's Government—every man of them. That is the will of Parliament and the nation. The British Empire and the French Republic, linked together in their cause and in their need, will defend to the death their native soil, aiding each other like good comrades⑪ to the utmost of their strength. Even though large tracts of Europe and many old and famous States have fallen or may fall into the grip of the Gestapo and all the odious⑫ apparatus of Nazi rule, we shall not flag or fail. We shall go on to the end, we shall fight in France, we shall fight on the seas and oceans, we shall fight with growing confidence and growing strength in the air, we shall defend our Island, whatever the cost may be, we shall fight on the beaches, we shall fight on the landing grounds, we shall fight in the fields and in the streets, we shall fight in the hills; we shall never surrender, and even if, which I do not for a moment believe, this Island or a large part of it were subjugated⑬ and starving, then our Empire beyond the seas, armed and guarded by the British Fleet, would carry on the struggle, until, in God's good time, the New World, with all its power and might, steps forth to the rescue and the liberation of the old.

难句解析

①**incomparably** [ɪnˈkɒmprəbli] adv. 无比地；不能比较地

②**stringency** [ˈstrɪndʒənsi] n. 严格，紧迫，说服力；严格性；强度

③**suspicious** [səˈspɪʃəs] adj. 可疑的；猜疑的，怀疑的；多疑的

④**nuisance** [ˈnjuːsns] n. 妨害；讨厌的事物

⑤**befool** [bɪˈfuːl] vt. 愚弄，欺骗，糟蹋

⑥**malice** [ˈmælɪs] n. 恶意，恶感；怨恨

⑦**ingenuity** [ˌɪndʒəˈnjuːəti] n. 足智多谋，心灵手巧；独创性

⑧**stratagem** [ˈstrætədʒəm] n. 诡计，计谋；花招

⑨**outlandish** [aʊtˈlændɪʃ] adj. 古怪的，奇异的；异国风格的

⑩**neglect** [nɪˈglekt] *v.* 疏忽；忽视

⑪**comrade** [ˈkɒmreɪd] *n.* （尤指共患难的）朋友；战友，同志

⑫**odious** [ˈəʊdiəs] *adj.* 可憎的，讨厌的，令人作呕的

⑬**subjugate** [ˈsʌbdʒugeɪt] *v.* 征服，降伏

难句解析

1. The whole question of home defense against invasion is, of course, powerfully affected by the fact that we have for the time being in this Island incomparably more powerful military forces than we have ever had at any moment in this war or the last.

译文 抵御敌军入侵的整个本土防御问题，毫无疑问，会在很大程度上受到这一事实影响：我们现在本土上拥有的军事力量要远远比我们曾经任何时期都强大，无论是这场战争还是一战。

解析 本句主干部分为"The whole question ... is powerfully affected by the fact"；"the fact"之后的"that"引导一个同位语从句，对"the fact"的内容进行了解释和说明；"... more powerful military forces than..."则用比较级的形式表达了最高级的含义，表明此时的军队比以往任何时候都要强大，足以抵御入侵。

2. We have found it necessary to take measures of increasing stringency, not only against enemy aliens and suspicious characters of other nationalities, but also against British subjects who may become a danger or a nuisance should the war be transported to the United Kingdom.

译文 我们认为现在有必要采取措施提高警惕，不仅是为应对外敌和其他国家的潜在敌人，还有一些英国国民，如若战争降临我国本土，这些人会很难处理，也可能很危险。

解析 "it"在此处为形式宾语，之后的动词不定式作真正的宾语；"not only... but also..."译为"不但……而且……"。

3. Turning once again, and this time more generally, to the question of invasion, I would observe that there has never been a period in all these long centuries of which we boast when an absolute guarantee against invasion, still less against serious raids, could have been given to our people.

译文 再一次更全面地回到德国入侵的问题上，我发现，过去的几个世纪

以来，我们从来不敢向我们的人民保证，我们有绝对的力量抵御入侵，更不用说大型袭击。

[解析] "I would observe that..." 中的 "observe" 在此处译为 "发现"；"... all these long centuries of which we boast..." 中的 "which" 引导定语从句，修饰先行词 "all these long centuries"，"boast" 在此处译为 "吹嘘"。

4. I have, myself, full confidence that if all do their duty, if nothing is neglected, and if the best arrangements are made, as they are being made, we shall prove ourselves once again able to defend our Island home, to ride out the storm of war, and to outlive the menace of tyranny, if necessary for years, if necessary alone.

[译文] 我本人完全相信，只要每个人各尽其职，毫不疏忽，并继续像现在这样正确行事，我们将再一次证明我们有能力防御我们的本土家园，安然度过战争风暴，在法西斯暴政的威胁后继续生存。如果有必要的话，战斗将持续多年，如果有必要的话，我们将孤军奋战。

[解析] "I have, myself, full confidence that" 引导同位语从句，在同位语从句中用 "if all do their duty, if nothing is neglected, and if the best arrangements are made" 排比句式增强文章气势。

参考译文

我们将战斗到底（节选）

抵御敌军入侵的整个本土防御问题，毫无疑问，会在很大程度上受到这一事实影响：我们现在本土上拥有的军事力量要远远比我们曾经任何时期都强大，无论是这场战争还是一战。但这还不够，我们不能满足于防御战争。我们还要承担保护盟国的职责。我们必须再次重组并强化英国远征军，并任命英勇的罗尔德·高特为最高指挥官。这些在未来都会完成。在这期间，我们必须把本土防御状态提升到高等级，我们才能用最少的人员应对威胁最大的潜在进攻。我们现在就要开始行动。如果议院同意的话，我们可以轻易在机密会议上讨论这个话题。政府并不一定能够透露军事机密，但是我们愿意让大家自由谈论，尽管第二天敌人就会知道这些信息。同时政府愿意听取来自国家不同地区的下议院各议员的一些见解，并从中受益。我知道，我们将在此问题上做出一些决策，而国王陛下的政府将欣然同意。

我们认为现在有必要采取措施提高警惕，不仅是为应对外敌和其他国家的潜在敌人，还有一些英国国民，如若战争降临我国本土，这些人会很难处理，也可能很危险。我知道，有许多人只是受我们政令鼓动，急切想要与纳粹德国作战。我只能对这些人表达歉意，但现在，处于当前的危机下，我们很难再像原本那样区分出这两个群体。如果凶残的敌人尝试空降英国，那么这群求战心切者最好还是远离激战，这样对他们自己和我们都好。不过，对于另外一个群体，那群真正的叛国者，我不会有一丁点儿同情。议会已经授权我们用强硬手段摧毁一切间谍活动（原文为"第五纵队"），我们也会用这些权力毫不犹豫地监督和纠正议院，直到我们满意为止，或更进一步，直到彻底消灭我们之间的毒瘤。

再一次更全面地回到德国入侵的问题上，我发现，过去的几个世纪以来，我们从来不敢向我们的人民保证，我们有绝对的力量抵御入侵，更不用说大型袭击。在拿破仑时代，他幻想有一阵风会带他的运输舰队跨越英吉利海峡，并驱散我们的封锁舰队。总会有这么个机会，而正是这种幻想，刺激欺骗了一个又一个欧洲大陆的暴君。这种事情，许多只能是停留在口头上的传说。我们可以确信，这种题材的小说会继续不断产生，我们可以从中看到我们敌人憎恨挑衅的独特创造力。当然，我们也要对任何小说策略和残忍奸诈的诡计做好准备。我觉得应该没有什么思想能如此神奇，值得我们去深入调查，但是同时，我也希望大家睁大眼睛。我们绝不能忘记英国海上力量和本地训练的空军对我们的坚定保证。

我本人完全相信，只要每个人各尽其职，毫不疏忽，并继续像现在这样正确行事，我们将再一次证明我们有能力防御我们的本土家园，安然度过战争风暴，在法西斯暴政的威胁后继续生存。如果有必要的话，战斗将持续多年，如果有必要的话，我们将孤军奋战。无论如何，这就是我们要做的事，这就是国王陛下的政府中每个人的决心，这就是我们议会和整个国家的意志。大英帝国和法兰西共和国在共同需求和利益下联合在一起誓死保卫国土，像生死战友一样尽最大的努力帮助彼此。即使欧洲的大量土地和许多知名的古老国家已经或即将沦陷在德国秘密警察和纳粹机构的统治之下，我们也丝毫不能动摇。我们将战斗到底，我们将在法国战斗，我们将在海洋上战斗，我们将以越来越坚定的决心和越来越强的力量在空中战斗，我们要保卫我们的本土，无论付出多大的代价。我们将在海滩上战斗，我们将在敌人的登陆地点战斗，我们将在田野和街道间战斗，我们将在山丘上战斗，我们绝不投降。即使我一点儿都不相信这种情况会发生，即使我们本土的大部分领土被敌人占领，并陷入饥荒，我们帝国在海外的领土在英国舰队的保护下，也会继续坚持战斗。直到上帝认为时机合适之时，新世界将以强大磅礴的力量前来拯救并解放这个旧世界。

读后写作

"We shall fight on the beaches" shows the firm confidence of Churchill. Can you tell us the reasons why he was so confident in the victory of the war?

The World As I See It
我的世界观
—— Albert Einstein

读前导语

本篇文章作者阿尔伯特·爱因斯坦（1879—1955），出生于德国符腾堡州乌尔姆市，毕业于苏黎世联邦理工学院，犹太裔物理学家，现代物理学的开创者、奠基人，被公认为是自伽利略、牛顿以来最伟大的科学家、物理学家。爱因斯坦提出光子假设，成功解释了光电效应，因此获得了1921年诺贝尔物理学奖。1905年创立狭义相对论，1915年创立广义相对论，1999年12月被《时代周刊》评选为"世纪伟人"。

他在文中写道："我实在是一个'孤独的旅客'，我未曾全心全意地属于我的国家、我的家庭、我的朋友，甚至我最为接近的亲人；在所有这些关系面前，我总是感觉到一定距离而且需要保持孤独——而这种感受正与年俱增。"

美文欣赏

What an extraordinary situation is that of us mortals[①]! Each of us is here for a brief sojourn[②]; for what purpose he knows not, though he sometimes thinks he feels it. But from the point of view of daily life, without going deeper, we exist for our fellow-men—in the first place for those on whose smiles and welfare all our happiness depends, and next for all those unknown to us personally with whose destinies we are bound up by the ties of sympathy. A hundred times every day I remind myself that my inner and outer life depend on the labours of other men, living and dead, and that I must exert[③] myself in order to give in the same measure as I have received and am still receiving. I am strongly drawn to the simple life and am often oppressed by the feeling that I am engrossing④ an unnecessary amount of the labour of my fellow-men. I regard class differences as contrary to justice and, in the last resort, based on force. I also consider that plain living is good for everybody, physically and mentally.

In human freedom in the philosophical sense I am definitely a disbeliever. Everybody acts not only under external compulsion but also in accordance with inner necessity. Schopenhauer's saying, that "a man can do as he will, but not will as he will," has been an inspiration to me since my youth, and a continual consolation and unfailing well-spring of patience in the face of the hardships of life, my own and others'. This feeling mercifully mitigates⑤ the sense of responsibility which so easily becomes paralyzing, and it prevents us from taking ourselves and other people too seriously; it conduces to a view of life in which humour, above all, has its due place.

To inquire after the meaning or object of one's own existence or of creation generally has always seemed to me absurd from an objective point of view. And yet everybody has certain ideals which determine the direction of his endeavors and his judgments. In this sense I have never looked upon ease and happiness as ends in themselves—such an ethical basis I call more proper for a herd of swine. The ideals which have lighted me on my way and time after time given me new courage to face life cheerfully, have been Truth, Goodness, and Beauty. Without the sense of fellowship with men of like mind, of preoccupation with the objective, the eternally unattainable in the field of art and scientific research, life would have seemed to me empty. The ordinary objects of human endeavor—property, outward success, luxury—have always seemed to me contemptible.

My passionate sense of social justice and social responsibility has always contrasted oddly with my pronounced freedom from the need for direct contact with other human beings and human communities. I am truly a "lone traveler" and have never belonged to my country, my home, my friends, or even my immediate family, with my whole heart; in the face of all these ties I have never lost an obstinate⑥ sense of detachment, of the need for solitude—a feeling which increases with the years. One is sharply conscious, yet without regret, of the limits to the possibility of mutual understanding and sympathy with one's fellow-creatures. Such a person no doubt loses something in the way of geniality and light-heartedness; on the other hand, he is largely independent of the opinions, habits, and judgments of his fellows and avoids the temptation to take his stand on such insecure foundations.

My political ideal is that of democracy. Let every man be respected as an individual and no man idolized. It is an irony of fate that I myself have been the recipient⑦ of excessive admiration and respect from my fellows through no fault, and no merit, of my own. The cause of this may well be the desire, unattainable for many, to understand the one or two ideas to which I have with my feeble powers attained through ceaseless struggle. I am quite aware that it is necessary for the success of any complex undertaking that one man should do the thinking and directing and in general bear the responsibility. But the led must not be compelled, they must be able to choose their leader. An autocratic system of coercion, in my opinion, soon degenerates⑧. For force always attracts men of low morality, and I believe it to be an invariable rule that tyrants of genius are succeeded by scoundrels. For this reason I have always been passionately opposed to systems such as we see in Italy and Russia today. The thing that has brought discredit upon the prevailing⑨ form of democracy in Europe today is not to be laid to the door of the democratic idea as such, but to lack of stability on the part of the heads of governments and to the impersonal character of the electoral system. I believe that in this respect the United States of America have found the right way. They have a responsible President who is elected for a sufficiently long period and has sufficient powers to be really responsible. On the other hand, what I value in our political system is the more extensive provision⑩ that it makes for the individual in case of illness or need. The really valuable thing in the pageant of human life seems to me not the State but the creative, sentient individual, the personality; it alone creates the noble and the sublime, while the herd as such remains dull in thought and dull in feeling.

This topic brings me to that worst outcrop of the herd nature, the military system, which I abhor. That a man can take pleasure in marching in formation to the strains of a band is enough to make me despise him. He has only been given his big brain by mistake; a backbone was all he needed. This plaguespot of civilization ought to be abolished with all possible speed. Heroism by order, senseless violence, and all the pestilent nonsense that does by the name of patriotism⑪—how I hate them! War seems to me a mean, contemptible thing: I would rather be hacked⑫ in pieces than take part in such an abominable⑬ business. And yet so high, in spite of everything, is my opinion of the human race that I believe this bogey would have disappeared long ago, had the sound sense of the nations not been systematically corrupted⑭ by commercial and political interests acting through the schools and the Press.

The fairest thing we can experience is the mysterious. It is the fundamental emotion which stands at the cradle⑮ of true art and true science. He who knows it not and can no longer wonder, no longer feel amazement, is as good as dead, a snuffed-out candle. It was the experience of mystery—even if mixed with fear—that engendered religion. A knowledge of the existence of something we cannot penetrate, of the manifestations⑯ of the profoundest reason and the most radiant⑰ beauty, which are only accessible to our reason in their most elementary forms—it is this knowledge and this emotion that constitute the truly religious attitude; in this sense, and in this alone, I am a deeply religious man. I cannot conceive⑱ of a God who rewards and punishes his creatures, or has a will of the type of which we are conscious in ourselves. An individual who should survive his physical death is also beyond my comprehension, nor do I wish it otherwise; such notions are for the fears or absurd egoism⑲ of feeble souls. Enough for me the mystery of the eternity of life, and the inkling of the marvelous structure of reality, together with the single-hearted endeavor to comprehend a portion, be it never so tiny, of the reason that manifests itself in nature.

词汇释义

① **mortal** ['mɔːtl] *n.* 凡人，普通人

② **sojourn** ['sɒdʒən] *n.* 逗留，旅居

③ **exert** [ɪɡ'zɜːt] *v.* 运用，施加；努力

④**engross** [ɪnˈgrəʊs] *v.* 使全神贯注

⑤**mitigate** [ˈmɪtɪgeɪt] *v.* 缓和，减轻；平息

⑥**obstinate** [ˈɒbstɪnət] *adj.* 顽固的；固执的；难以控制的

⑦**recipient** [rɪˈsɪpiənt] *n.* 接受者；容器；容纳者

⑧**degenerate** [dɪˈdʒenəreɪt] *v.* 恶化；衰退；堕落

⑨**prevailing** [prɪˈveɪlɪŋ] *adj.* 占优势的；普遍的；盛行的

⑩**provision** [prəˈvɪʒn] *n.* 规定，条项，条款；预备，准备

⑪**patriotism** [ˈpætriətɪzəm] *n.* 爱国主义；爱国心，爱国精神

⑫**hack** [hæk] *v.* 乱劈，乱砍

⑬**abominable** [əˈbɒmɪnəbl] *adj.* 讨厌的；令人极为不快的

⑭**corrupt** [kəˈrʌpt] *v.* 使堕落，使腐化；破坏

⑮**cradle** [ˈkreɪdl] *n.* 摇篮；发源地

⑯**manifestation** [ˌmænɪfeˈsteɪʃn] *n.* 表示，显示；示威

⑰**radiant** [ˈreɪdiənt] *adj.* 照耀的；辐射的；容光焕发的

⑱**conceive** [kənˈsiːv] *v.* 想象，构想；认为；怀孕

⑲**egoism** [ˈiːgəʊɪzəm] *n.* 自我主义；利己主义

难句解析

1. A hundred times every day I remind myself that my inner and outer life depend on the labours of other men, living and dead, and that I must exert myself in order to give in the same measure as I have received and am still receiving.

[译文] 我每天上百次地提醒自己：我的精神生活和物质生活都是以别人（包括生者和死者）的劳动为基础的，我必须尽力以同样的分量来报偿我所领受了的和至今还在领受着的东西。

[解析] "remind" 译为 "提醒"；两个 that 均引导宾语从句； "measure" 在此处译为 "分量"。

2. My passionate sense of social justice and social responsibility has always contrasted oddly with my pronounced freedom from the need for direct contact with other human beings and human communities.

【译文】 我有强烈的社会正义感和社会责任感，但我又明显地缺乏与别人和社会直接接触的要求，这两者总是形成古怪的对照。

【解析】 "the sense of" 译为 "……的感觉"；"contrast" 在此处译为 "对比；显出明显的差异"，是动词。

3. An individual who should survive his physical death is also beyond my comprehension, nor do I wish it otherwise; such notions are for the fears or absurd egoism of feeble souls. Enough for me the mystery of the eternity of life, and the inkling of the marvelous structure of reality, together with the single-hearted endeavor to comprehend a portion, be it never so tiny, of the reason that manifests itself in nature.

【译文】 我不能也不愿去想象一个人在肉体死亡以后还会继续活着；让那些脆弱的灵魂，由于恐惧或者由于可笑的唯我论，去拿这种思想当宝贝吧！我自己只求满足于生命永恒的奥秘，满足于觉察现存世界的神奇结构，窥见它的一鳞半爪，并且以诚挚的努力去领悟在自然界中显示出来的那个理性的一部分，倘若真能如此，即使只领悟其极小的一部分，我也就心满意足了。

【解析】 "beyond my comprehension" 本义为 "超出了我的理解"，此处译为 "我不愿意"；"notion" 在此处译为 "概念，观念"；"together with" 译为 "和……一起"。

参考译文

我的世界观

我们这些总有一死的人的命运多么奇特！我们每个人在这个世界上都只作一个短暂的逗留；目的何在，却无从知道，尽管有时自以为对此若有所感。但是，不必深思，只要从日常生活就可以明白：人是为别人而生存的——首先是为那样一些人，我们的幸福全部依赖于他们的喜悦和健康；其次是为许多我们所不认识的人，他们的命运通过同情的纽带同我们密切结合在一起。我每天上百次地提醒自己：我的精神生活和物质生活都是以别人（包括生者和死者）的劳动为基础的，我必须尽力以同样的分量来报偿我所领受了的和至今还在领受着的东西。我强烈地向往着俭朴的生活，并且时常发觉自己占用了同胞的过多劳动而难以忍受。我认为阶级的区分是不合理的，它最后所凭借的是以暴力为根据。我也相信，简单淳朴的生活，无论在身体上还是在精神上，对每个人都是有益的。

我完全不相信人类会有那种在哲学意义上的自由。每一个人的行为不仅受着外界的强制，而且要适应内在的必然。叔本华说："人虽然能够做他所想做的，但不能要他所想要的。"这句格言从我青年时代起就给了我真正的启示；在我自己和别人的生活面临困难的时候，它总是使我们得到安慰，并且是宽容的持续不断的源泉。这种体会可以宽大为怀地减轻那种容易使人气馁的责任感，也可以防止我们过于严肃地对待自己和别人；它导致一种特别给幽默以应有地位的人生观。

要追究一个人自己或一切生物生存的意义或目的，从客观的观点看来，我总觉得是愚蠢可笑的。可是每个人都有一些理想，这些理想决定着他的努力和判断的方向。就在这个意义上，我从来不把安逸和享乐看作生活目的本身——我把这种伦理基础叫作猪栏的理想。照亮我的道路，并且不断地给我新的勇气去愉快地正视生活的理想，是真、善和美。要是没有志同道合者之间的亲切感情，要不是全神贯注于客观世界——那个在艺术和科学工作领域里永远达不到的对象，那么在我看来，生活就会是空虚的。我总觉得，人们所努力追求的庸俗目标——财产、虚荣、奢侈的生活——都是可鄙的。

我有强烈的社会正义感和社会责任感，但我又明显地缺乏与别人和社会直接接触的要求，这两者总是形成古怪的对照。我实在是一个"孤独的旅客"，我未曾全心全意地属于我的国家、我的家庭、我的朋友，甚至我最为接近的亲人；在所有这些关系面前，我总是感觉到一定距离而且需要保持孤独——而这种感受正与年俱增。人们会清楚地发觉，同别人的相互了解和协调一致是有限度的，但这不值得惋惜。无疑，这样的人在某种程度上会失去他的天真无邪和无忧无虑的心境；但另一方面，他却能够在很大程度上不为别人的意见、习惯和判断所左右，并且能够避免那种把他的内心平衡建立在这样一些不可靠的基础之上的诱惑。

我的政治理想是民主政体。让每一个人都作为个人而受到尊重，而不让任何人成为被崇拜的偶像。我自己一直受到同代人的过分的赞扬和尊敬，这不是由于我自己的过错，也不是由于我自己的功劳，而实在是一种命运的嘲弄。其原因大概在于人们有一种愿望，想理解我以自己微薄的绵力，通过不断的斗争所获得的少数几个观念，而这种愿望有很多人却未能实现。我完全明白，一个组织要实现它的目的，就必须有一个人去思考、去指挥，并且全面担负起责任来。但是被领导的人不应当受到强迫，他们必须能够选择自己的领袖。在我看来，强迫的专制制度很快就会腐化堕落。因为暴力所招引来的总是一些品德低劣的人，而且我相信，天才的暴君总是由无赖来继承的，这是一条千古不易的规律。就是由于这个缘故，我总强烈地反对今天在意大利和俄国所见到的那种制度。像欧洲今天所存在的情况，已使得民主形式受到怀疑，这不能归咎于民主原则本身，而是由于政府的不稳定和选举制度中与个人无关的特征。我相信美国在这方面已经找到了正确的道路。他们选出了一个任期足够长的总统，他有充分的权力来真正履行他的职责。另一方面，在德国政治制度中，为我所看重的是它为救济患病或贫困的人做出了比较广泛的规定。在人生的丰富多彩的表演中，我觉得真正可贵的，不是政治上的国家，而是有创造性的、有感情的个人，是人格；只有个人才能创造出高尚的和卓越的东西，而群众本身在思想上总是迟钝的，在感觉上也总是迟钝的。

讲到这里，我想起了群众生活中最坏的一种表现，那就是使我厌恶的军事制度。一个人能够扬扬得意地随着军乐队在四列纵队里行进，单凭这一点就足以使我对他鄙夷不屑。他所以长了一个大脑，只是出于误会；光是骨髓就可满足他的全部需要了。文明的这种罪恶的渊薮，应当尽快加以消灭。任人支配的英雄主义、冷酷无情的暴行，以及在爱国主义名义下的一切可恶的胡闹，所有这些都使我深恶痛绝！在我看来，战争是多么卑鄙、下流！我宁愿被千刀万剐，也不愿参与这种可憎的勾当。尽管如此，我对人类的评价还是十分高的，我相信，要是人民的健康感情没有遭到那些通过学校和报纸而起作用的商业利益和政治利益的蓄意败坏，那么战争这个妖魔早就该绝迹了。

我们所能有的最美好的经验是奥秘的经验。它是坚守在真正艺术和真正科学发源地上的基本感情。谁要是体验不到它，谁要是不再有好奇心，也不再有惊讶的感觉，谁就无异于行尸走肉，他的眼睛便是模糊不清的。就是这样奥秘的经验——虽然掺杂着恐惧——产生了宗教。我们认识到有某种为我们所不能洞察的东西存在，感觉到那种只能以其最原始的形式接近我们的心灵的最深奥的理性和最灿烂的美——正是这种认识和这种情感构成了真正的宗教感情；在这个意义上，而且也只是在这个意义上，我才是一个具有深挚的宗教感情的人。我无法想象存在这样一个上帝，它会对自己的创造物加以赏罚，会具有我们在自己身上所体验到的那种意志。我不能也不愿去想象一个人在肉体死亡以后还会继续活着；让那些脆弱的灵魂，由于恐惧或者由于可笑的唯我论，去拿这种思想当宝贝吧！我自己只求满足于生命永恒的奥秘，满足于觉察现存世界的神奇结构，窥见它的一鳞半爪，并且以诚挚的努力去领悟在自然界中显示出来的那个理性的一部分，倘若真能如此，即使只领悟其极小的一部分，我也就心满意足了。

读后写作

Different people have different perspectives to look at the world. What is the world in your eyes?